Chautauqua:
Its Architecture
and Its People

Enjoy!,
Pauline Faucher

Chautauqua:
Its Architecture
and Its People

by Pauline Fancher

Banyan Books, Inc.
Miami, Florida

Contents

The arrival of the Chautauqua Lake
Steamer, "City of Buffalo" at the boat
landing near the Miller Bell Tower,
about 1921.

Illustrations

Baggage on Pier, 1916.

Preface

In 1872, Lewis Miller said to Mrs. Kate P. Bruch of Canton, Ohio, and her sister, "Girls, why would it not be a good thing to have a Sunday School Camp Meeting?" That same year Mr. Miller and John Vincent began Chautauqua at the location of the previously existing Erie Conference Camp-Meeting Association. Chautauqua is now a world-famous religious, educational, and recreational colony that has carried its message to all nations.

This book presents a picture of Chautauqua then and now. Part I, First Century, portrays the forces that made us the way we are. I have attempted to provide historical information on some typical Chautauquan structures, to relate how our surroundings changed as decades passed, and to tell something about the contributions of our residents and visitors. What is presented is, of necessity, but a selection. There is much more of significance to be described, and it is my hope that a subsequent book will follow.

Much of the unique charm of Chautauqua lies in its setting of nineteenth-century buildings, mainly of Gothic Revival, Eastlake, Vernacular, and Gingerbread types. Most of those described were chosen by Buffalo architect Olaf William Shelgren as typical Chautauqua architecture. They form the basis of Chautauqua's becoming a Historic Site.

Buildings accepted as National Landmarks and Historic Sites are considered the most significant ones in the United States. One advantage in being so designated is that public funds may not be used to demolish the buildings except under exceptional circumstances.

Early Chautauqua emphasized Classical architecture, and it is important that our historic buildings be preserved. For example, in the center of old Chautauqua at Miller and Clark stands an example of Italianate architecture, a type prominent in the Victorian period. It was our first Administration Building, then the Assembly Herald building, later Halaby's Bazaar; it is now Dean's Bazaar. I feel strongly that this building should not be torn down to make way for a modern structure.

I have tried to set up guidelines for evaluating what is traditionally "Chautauquesque" and makes us distinctive. It is my hope that this book may be taken on walks for a greater appreciation of our architecture and of the generations of notable and interesting persons who have lived and visited within our gate.

Chautauqua was placed on the National Register of Historic Places in 1972. This led to its becoming a New York State Historic Site on June 19, 1973. To accomplish the latter, a Site Survey of the houses and buildings within the gate – over seven hundred of them – was conducted during our Centennial year. A Site Survey Committee of over sixty members, under my direction, compiled all of the information necessary for our application.

Every street was photographed, and many of the photographs taken are used in Part II, Second Century, of this book. We acknowledge with thanks the Peacock Landmark Society and the William Millers, Jr., for providing financial assistance to the committee for the photography. Senator Jesse J. Present and Steven Levy of the New York State Historic Trust were invaluable in aiding us to become a Historic Site. Mr. Levy presented our application to the New York State Council of Parks and recreation. The presentation of the Historic Site certificate took place in the Hall of Philosophy on July 21, 1973.

Chautauqua is a place that I continue to love, as do countless residents and visitors. It is my hope that the reader will, too, appreciate it even more through the information offered in the forthcoming pages.

Acknowledgments

The author wishes to thank all who helped in the preparation of this book, first, my glorious family who always believed in me no matter how impossible seem the tasks I undertake.

Next, thanks to all my many friends who spurred me on and gave me moral support; these include Bess, Alice, and Bette as well as Margaret Copeland and Margaret Miller Newman, who introduced me to the human side of Chautauqua as well as the factual.

Special thanks go to the Smith Memorial Library staff for their interest and encouragement, and to those who read and commented on my manuscript.

To the Peacock Landmark Society I owe a debt of gratitude. They never fail to further interest in preserving the historical treasures of our county and they helped financially with the survey and this book.

Professional advice was given me by Bill Shelgren and by the firm of Naetzker, Thorsell, & Gostomski. My teacher, Dr. Daniel D. Reiff, instructed me in the glories of architecture at the State University of New York at Fredonia.

Thanks go to Si, Rosemary, Carol, Doug, Nancy, and Chris who took pictures for the survey.

Finally, to the survey committee, who spent endless hours in the attic of the County Court House checking dates of houses, who walked Chautauqua streets tirelessly with historic forms, and who were instrumental in our being placed on the National Register. A list of their names follows:

Marjorie Jenkins

Dr. Walter Dunn Jr.

Buffalo Historical Soc.

Buffalo, N.Y.

Mrs. Helen Thurston

Mrs. Ralph Loomis

Mina Arnn

Mrs. Eleanor Carter

Mr. and Mrs. John Doig

Mrs. Helen Theurer

Mr. and Mrs. Maury Knowlton

Clare Lindberg

Mr. and Mrs. D. C. Duncan

Mrs. Howard Minor

Mr. and Mrs. George Cleveland

Mrs. Robert Griewahn

Mrs. Lucile Parsons

Mrs. Jean Voltman

Mrs. R. H. Eckhardt

Miss Judy McCandless

Miss Linda Hinzman

Mrs. Gladis Funk

Mr. H. Harper

Mrs. Russell Arnold

Mrs. B. C. Giffords

Mrs. Joseph Mihm

Mrs. J. D. Rice

Mr. and Mrs. H. R. Duhme and Warren

Mrs. Frank Karslake

Miss Helen Estabrook

Mrs. William E. Miller, Jr.

Mrs. Bartlett Richards

Mrs. Priscilla Nixon

Dr. and Mrs. Carl Winters

John Malcolm

Mr. Kenneth Baker

Hotel Wm. Baker

Mr. Howard Gibbs

Miss Rosemary Rappole

Mr. Ralph Moore

Virginia Cushman

Mrs. Richard Hipple

Miss Becky Reading

Betsy Morgan

Mrs. Bailey

Miss Mary Ann McMillan

Mr. David Caldwell

Mrs. Helen Lockwood

Mr. Roy Uptegraff, Jr.

Mrs. Allen Rice

Mrs. Arthur Seeback, Sr.

Miss Ruth Irwin

Mrs. George Evans

Mrs. Paul Branch

Mrs. Wm. Piper

Nathalie Leonard

Mrs. George Cornell

Mr. Jack Dean

Mrs. Laughlin

Mrs. Robert Coblenz

Mrs. Margaret Miller Newman

Mrs. Margaret Dochterman

Mrs. Mary Meisse

Mrs. Hugh Mack Dill

This is a personal book written by a Chautauquan for Chautauquans and would-be Chautauquans. I hope you like it.

Longfellow Cottage, 1885.

I
First
Century

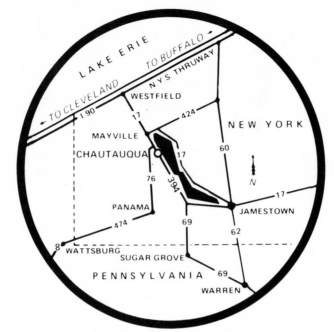

Map showing New York, Pennsylvania, and Ohio.

Introduction

Nestled in groves of trees in New York state is an emerald lake called Chautauqua. George Washington, just before he became president, was called to face the problem of ready communication between East and West. He thought the route by Lake Chautauqua might be the solution. In 1788 he wrote, "If the Chautauqua Lake at the head of the Conewango River approximates Lake Erie as near as it is laid down in the draft you sent me, it presents a very short portage between the two and access to all those above the latter."[1]

Even though it did not meet Washington's expectations, the area has long been known as a Gateway to the West. It has gained world prominence through Chautauqua Institution and the "Chautauqua Idea."

Chautauqua Lake is located in western New York with Mayville at its head and Jamestown at the outlet. It narrows near its center at Bemus Point. Many people believe that its name comes from the Indian word "Chautauqua," which in some sign languages is interpreted as "bag tied in the middle."

Originally called Fair Point, Chautauqua Institution is located on the lake three miles south of Mayville. Set among gently sloping hills with fields and foliage on all sides, it is regarded as one of the most beautiful locations on the lake.

Chautauqua was the idea of two men, Lewis Miller and John Heyl Vincent.

Lewis Miller was born July 24, 1829 at Greentown, Ohio. At the age of 16 he was a schoolteacher. In 1849 he worked at the plastering trade. Mr. Miller invented the Buckeye Mower and Reaper. This invention made him famous and, perhaps more importantly, it provided funds for him to pursue his humanitarian interest in education and religion. As a Methodist Sunday School superintendent in Akron, Ohio, he early organized a normal class to train young people to teach in his school.

John Heyl Vincent became Secretary of Sunday School work for the Methodist denomination in 1868 and often came in contact with Mr. Miller in planning an early normal course. He was a descendant of the Huguenot migrants to America during the persecutions of Louis XIV.

Born on February 23, 1832 in Tuscaloosa, Alabama, Vincent taught in the Lewisburg, Pennsylvania public schools at the age of 15. He later was licensed in the Methodist Episcopal Church and in 1853 was received as a member "on trial" in the New Jersey Conference. Camptown, New Jersey, was his second charge. Here he established a definitive course of Bible teaching for teachers and young people. He conducted the lessons of the Palestine Class with the germ of an idea that may have developed into Chautauqua's Palestine Park—the replica of the Holy Land in Miller Park.

After four years in New Jersey Vincent transferred to the Illinois Conference. At Galena, Illinois, Ulysses S. Grant was a member of his congregation. Later, during his Chicago pastorate, he introduced a uniform lesson in the schools of the city. He was called to become the first General Agent of the Sunday School Union of the Methodist Sunday Schools throughout the world. In 1868, Dr. Vincent became its Secretary and Editor.

The Fair Point landing in 1874 was
practically untouched by human hand.

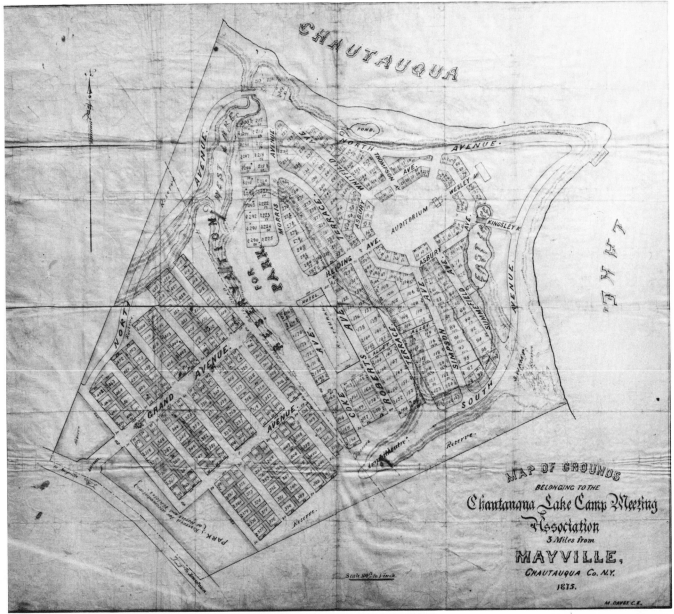

This 1875 map shows the original purchase from the Camp Meeting Association.

Founders Lewis Miller and John Vincent.

The Auditorium of the Camp Meeting group was used by the Chautauqua Assembly in 1874, but was soon outgrown.

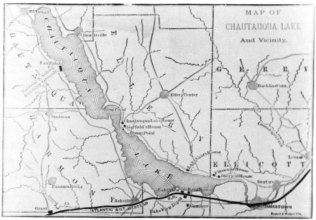
A map of Chautauqua Lake and vicinity showing Fair Point on the upper left side of the lake.

How Chautauqua Began

George Vincent, the nine-year-old son of cofounder John Heyl Vincent, claims that he discovered Chautauqua. He was the first ashore when Lewis Miller, his son Ira, and George's father, Bishop Vincent, visited Chautauqua, then known as Fair Point. Quite appropriately, George Vincent later became one of Chautauqua's presidents.

Lewis Miller was a trustee of the Sunday School Assembly held at the Fair Point Camp Ground, then in the charge of Dr. W. W. Wythe. It was Mr. Miller who persuaded John Vincent to come and see the attractive site where he believed an outdoor school for Sunday School teachers would thrive. Bishop Vincent, when he arrived by boat from Mayville, was so pleased by the beauty of the point that jutted out into Chautauqua Lake that he willingly gave up his idea of a conference in a metropolitan area.

Vincent established his office in Plainfield, New Jersey. He became the editor of the *Sunday School Journal,* the teachers' magazine of his church. This journal soon reached a circulation of 200,000. With his exciting voice and his "pen of fire," he appealed everywhere for a training that should fit Sunday School teachers for their great work.

He established normal classes in many places, charting courses of instruction for students. He thought that students should receive more benefit from a fortnight in daily study than in six months of weekly meetings. He felt there should be lectures on inspiring themes plus a spice of entertainment.

Vincent and Miller became kindred spirits. Miller's practical, wise genius proved the perfect leveler for Vincent's idealistic plans. Vincent's vision was for a city conference, Miller's an outdoor place for a conference.

Together they set forth their objectives in what is known as the "Chautauqua Idea."

The Chautauqua Idea.

The whole of life is a school, with educating influences all the while at work. These agencies and influences should be wisely and continuously applied by and in behalf of each individual. Intellectual activity must be continuous in order to promote intellectual health and efficiency. Chautauqua provides a school for people out of school, who can no longer attend school, a college for one's own home, and leads to the dedication of everyday life to educational purposes. The work is so carefully planned that by doing a little every day and following the weekly outline which is provided, the reader makes his odd moments tell to the best advantage. Reading, reading, reading, page after page, chapter after chapter, book after book, one may gradually become absorbed in elevating themes, gain knowledge and power, brighten life, strengthen character, broaden one's world, and come into fellowship and kinship with noble souls. Thus the reader improves the conversation at the fireside, sets a good example to the children and neighbors, trains the will power, and keeps the soul from deteriorating under the worry and hurry of this busy age.

How They Came

The welcoming gate at Chautauqua was far different in the early days when patrons of the Assembly entered by steamboat, train, or horse and buggy. Guests landed by steamers from Mayville and Jamestown with everything from satchels to rakes. President Grant arrived aboard the *Dixie Bell* when he came to visit in 1875.

In 1878, people came to Mayville via the Pennsylvania Railroad and then to Fair Point by boat. From Jamestown they arrived on the Atlantic and Great Western with hourly runs by boat. A railroad station at the foot of Harris Avenue accommodated arrivals by the Buffalo, N. Y. and Pennsylvania Railroad. It was an all-day trip from Jamestown to Chautauqua behind horse but less than three hours by boat.

No matter how you arrived at Chautauqua, your entrance fee was paid at a gate. This entitled you to attendance to activities on the grounds. You showed your ticket when you left, however, even as one does today.

Rudyard Kipling, in his book, *Abaft the Funnel,* describes his entrance to Chautauqua in the chapter "Chautauquaed":

I can't hope to give you an idea of it, but try to imagine the Charlesville at Mussorie magnified ten times and set down in the midst of hundreds of tiny little hill houses each different from its neighbour, brightly painted and constructed of wood. Add something of the peace of dull Dalhousie, flavour with a tincture of missions and the old Polytechnic, Cassell's Self Educator and a Monday pop, and spread the result out flat on the shores of Naini Tal Lake, which you will please transport to the Dun. But that does not half describe the idea. We watched it through a wicket gate, where we were furnished with a red ticket, price forty cents, and five dollars if you lost it. I naturally lost mine and was fined accordingly.

Once inside the grounds on the paths that serpentined round the myriad cottages I was lost in admiration of scores of pretty girls, most of them with little books under their arms, and a pretty air of seriousness on their faces."[2]

His exit was not so pleasant, for his friend had left the grounds with his ticket. Mr. Kipling continues: "The trouble began when I attempted to escape through the wicket on the jetty and let the creeds fight it out among themselves. Without that ticket I could not go, unless I paid five dollars."[3]

Mr. Kipling was forced to pay the five dollars. It all ended well as his friend returned with Kipling's ticket and recovered the money.

4

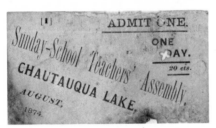

A ticket was purchased for $5 for the season, and patrons had to show it upon arrival and departure. The same holds true today.

The old road gate was made of wood.

What They Saw

The main entrance to Chautauqua in the 1870s was by Chautauqua Lake, and the area around the point was the first to be settled. Gradually, cottages and buildings were erected up the hill to what is now Bestor Plaza. The early area or "Old Chautauqua" extended from North Avenue to South Avenue. In 1877, the name was changed from Fair Point to Chautauqua.

One of the first uses of visual aids in education was Palestine Park, an outdoor relief map of the Holy Land. It was located on the left as you entered the Point from the boat. It was made for the First Assembly by the Rev. W. W. Wythe.

The points of the compass are in reverse and Chautauqua Lake takes the place of the Mediterranean Sea with the principal mountains, valleys, watercourses, and cities shown by metal plaques. The scale of distances on the model was about one and three-quarters feet per mile, and it covered a distance of 300 feet. The model is made of earth and is covered with grass.

Although Palestine Park was meant to be temporary, it continued to be of interest. One Chautauqua president remarked that "Every year I get letters asking how long it will take to drive around Palestine Park."

Nature startled the early Fair Point patrons by spouting water out of a tree. This unusual spring was located at the point near the Boat Landing. The map of 1883 shows a well on the point. There was also a pump on Center Avenue. Marion Thomas, a veteran Chautauquan who began her Chautauqua summers in 1898, relates that bottled water was obtainable at the Beaujean Cottage on Terrace Avenue.

An 1880 view of the Choir on Palestine Park.

5

A phenomenon was a tree that spouted water (with a little help from human nature). Oriental House, an early museum, is shown in the background.

The first outdoor lighting was found at Chautauqua. As early as 1883, Miller Park was aglow with street lamps.

A classical lady kept vigil in the grove near Fair Point landing.

There was a candy stand on the point from 1874-1880. It had "a full line of confects." According to the *Assembly Herald,* "Mr. Allen, the owner, has everything which a sweet tooth could crave or a delicate palate desire. Try his hot candy, warm peanuts, fresh popcorn or something else, everything worth tasting."

The Massey clan gathered under their tent.

Types of Architecture Found at Chautauqua

Since nineteenth-century architecture is considered the typical American style, Chautauqua architecture is typically American. Its houses and buildings, presented in chronological order, are important in preserving the "Chautauquaesque Look" which makes it unique.

Many nineteenth-century styles popular at Chautauqua carried over into the twentieth century. New ones were introduced. Attempts have been made to encourage cottage holders to replace wood with wood rather than cement or wrought iron. Blending the houses and buildings into the Victorian setting is also encouraged.

Culture started under canvas with Frank Beard of *Judge Magazine* captivating an audience with his sketches.

TENTS

Many early Chautauquans lived in tents or tent houses. Tents were often brought to Chautauqua by visitors; some were made on the grounds, others were rented. Ads for renting tents appeared in the Chautauqua *Assembly Herald.* Many large tents were purchased from the World's Fair in Philadelphia in 1876. They were used not only for sleeping quarters but also for meeting places.

As late as 1891 houses were constructed on tent platforms, with no basements underneath but with crawl spaces provided. The house at 34 Janes Avenue still maintains its platform and has a space in the foundation where a small individual may crawl underneath if necessary. As a matter of fact, it once came in mighty handy when a skunk died under the house.

7

The tent idea was copied by Thousand Island Park and other Chautauquas from the "Mother Chautauqua."

The Vincent Cottage at 36 S. Lake Drive had a striped tent covering a cupolalike porch.

The rambling Arcade combined Victorian characteristics including gables, porches, sawn art, and decorations.

VICTORIAN (1837-1901)

"Victorian" is associated with the region of Queen Victoria. Richness of ornament, characteristic of the Second Empire-French, is also identified with the term "Victorian." The vertical lines are similar to the Italianate and Gothic. Frame houses with steep roofs and flat walls were embellished with intricate decoration of gables, porches, and window lintels. The trend toward originality and novelty of decoration qualified as "picturesque."

8

The McKee-Karslake house with Greek Revival qualities boasted Ionic columned porches overlooking the lake.

GREEK REVIVAL (1815-1840)

Greek Revival architecture had passed its peak when Chautauqua was founded. Elements of the Classical are seen in such buildings as the Hall of Philosophy and the Hall of Christ.

Fine Greek details may be found on many private homes. Columns, capitals, and low-gabled pediments, typical characteristics, may be seen, but few Greek temples. Some houses had shifted the long side of the portico to the gabled end.

Classical columns held up Classical entablatures with pedimented gables. Some had columned entrance porticos and vertical windows. This style was beyond the reach of the average middle-class Chautauquan.

The McKee-Karslake house on South Lake Drive is a beautiful example of this type of architecture, which was popular earlier in western New York.

GOTHIC REVIVAL (1835-1880)

It seems only fitting that Gothic Revival structures that recaptured the romance of medieval buildings were used in the picturesque Chautauqua setting. The typical vertical effect produced through sharp pointed gables with slender finials at the peaks could easily be adapted to long, narrow building lots. In religious Chautauqua they made your eyes travel heavenward.

Tall and slender windows adapted well to narrow lots and buildings. Casement windows with leaded diamond-shaped panes were a favorite. Wooden verge boards under the eaves had a heyday. Many wooden motifs were precut and were often purchased from catalogs.

Englishman A. J. Downing's *Architecture for Country Houses*[4] was widely used as a model in America and was reflected in Chautauqua's Gothic houses. The simple gatehouses pictured in his book formed the basis for many local cottages. Since many carpenters designed their own houses, they relied on carpenter handbooks such as Calvert Vaux's *Villas and Cottages* and William T. Comstock and A. J. Bicknell's *Modern Architectural Designs and Details.* Carpenter's lace could be bought by the yard. Gothic Revival is also called Carpenter Gothic, Steamboat Gothic, and American Gothic.

The Little White House at 17 Roberts Avenue shows the results of the imagination of a carpenter craftsman in the delicate design of the balustrade and the bargeboard decorations in the gables.

9

Long verandas are a feature of the Swiss type cottage at 28 Miller Park, which was the adaptation of Gothic Revival style employed in the Miller and Massey cottages.

SWISS COTTAGE (OFFSHOOT OF GOTHIC REVIVAL)

Since "picturesque" is the outstanding quality of a cottage in the Swiss manner, it is not surprising that it found its way to Chautauqua. This type dwelling is also interesting because Lewis Miller chose it for his home.

An offspring of Gothic Revival, it shows a great deal of ornamental work in the brackets that support the roof as well as the borders of the doors and windows. The Miller Cottage follows this pattern with a decorative piece of stick art in the roof peak, which is bracketed. A Swiss cottage is built off the ground so that animals may be housed underneath. It is usually built on a hillside, and this may have been why Mr. Miller chose this particular type.

A long veranda is another characteristic that aptly applies to the Miller Cottage. Broad roofs, open galleries, and simple, bold construction are significant of strength and fitness, which may be another explanation of why he chose this adaptation of Gothic Revival.

ITALIANATE (1845-1885)

The Italianate or Tuscan Villa style resembled medieval Italian villas. The sloped, overhanging roof was supported by scrolled brackets of wood. Sometimes the squared shapes and lines included a tower or campanile, or an observatory on the center of the roof. Miller Bell Tower is such a campanile or bell tower.

Flat-topped and round-topped windows often had elaborate decorations. Square-pillared porches with semicircular arches, another Italianate characteristic, are found at Dean's Bazaar. Italianate qualities are combined in many Vernacular type buildings on the grounds, giving openness and easy access to the view.

Curved arches and banding, which break the columns holding them up, designate the Administration Building as "Italianate" and "Victorian."

Stick style employed numerous pieces of light wood. Eastlake was a carpenter's version of stick style. This is the Follansbee House at 13-1/2 Foster.

Second Empire, or Mansard, at 5-7 Morris. The mansard roof was popular at Chautauqua because it gave extra space.

STICK STYLE

Stick style originated before 1860 and used the balloon frame construction that employed numerous pieces of light wood. The Follansbee house at 13-1/2 Foster is a charming example of stick style technique. This mode was used in Swiss architecture, and we see a suggestion of it in the Miller Cottage.

EASTLAKE

Eastlake is often suggested as the proper term of much of Chautauqua architecture. The main difference between stick style and Eastlake is that it has less of a general sense of banding and more isolated details such as bargeboard and braces.

This style was named after architect Charles Lock Eastlake, author of *Hints on Household Taste in Furniture, Upholstery, and Other Details* (1868).[5] Professor Daniel Reiff, in his book, *Architecture in Fredonia,* aptly comments: "In a way the style is a carpenter's version of the Stick style, since the sort of decoration natural to wood (turning and gouging) comes to the fore."[6] Some people feel that all of the Chautauqua Grounds is Eastlake, others confine themselves to a single example such as 8 Vincent.

SECOND EMPIRE OR MANSARD (1855-1885)

Second Empire or Mansard Style may be recognized by the steep slope of the roof. Extra living space (often at a premium at Chautauqua, as in Paris, where it originated) was gained on the top floor by bending out the shape of the roof. Dormers allowed the entrance of light and broke the monotony of the uppermost level. The dormers were often ornamented with pediments and the roof bracketed.

The style, especially adaptable to commercial buildings, was introduced during the reign of Napoleon III (1852-1870). It took its name from the man who introduced it, Francois Mansart. The house at 5-7 Morris Avenue is an interesting rendition of this style.

11

The pictorial quality of the Methodist House, 14 Pratt, rambling and with a corner tower, designates it as Queen Anne style.

QUEEN ANNE (1875-1900)

The quality of the Queen Anne style fits into the pictorial setting of Chautauqua and adapts itself to its stately houses. Round corner towers form a prominent part of the Methodist House on Pratt and Bowman, as do the turrets on the Booth house at 46 S. Lake and the house at 39 Janes Avenue. Elaborately turned posts add to the Doeright house at 30 Peck and the sawn art shingles enhance the cottage.

These cottages combine a variety of shapes and textures into a pleasing whole in the Queen Anne manner. The porches feature delicate spindlework and horizontal bands. The typical clapboard of Chautauqua is mixed with smooth boards and shingles. This style uses gables, dormers, chimneys, round turrets, and oriel and stained glass windows. Terra cotta is employed for decoration. Fluted brick chimneys with large caps are used. A nonsymmetrical composition of shapes and textures combine into a pleasant cottage exterior.

Smith Memorial Library, at Clark and Miller, was built in 1931. It has Georgian lines and is constructed of red brick with white wood trim.

NEO-GEORGIAN (1920-1930)

Several Georgian style influences may be found on the grounds. Many of the robust details characterizing Georgian style were carefully blended into the facade. Neo-Gothic and Neo-Georgian were popular styles on campuses in the 1920s and 30s.

Georgian style used doorways surrounded by pilasters or columns, surmounted by cornices or pediments. Often, there was a semicircular fanlight over the door. Classical elements were refined into thin and attenuated forms. Palladian or triple windows on the second floor were popular. Window cornices had window caps. A projecting entrance pavilion was often topped by a pedimented gable. Corners on masonry houses usually had stone quoins.

Many Georgian buildings were of brick construction with white wooden trim. The Georgian-style woodwork of the interior was often as lavish as the exterior details. Smith Library combines many of these characteristics, and Packard Manor has Adam friezes in its interior.

CONTEMPORARY

Since "Contemporary" houses employ no set historic pattern, many houses at the north and south ends of the grounds follow this style. Structures built in the twentieth century adapt to the larger lots and are consequently more spacious.

Another outstanding characteristic is the use of natural materials such as brick, stone, or wood. This use is much more in evidence in the twentieth-century houses on the grounds.

The Christopher Norton House at 1 Packard Manor is built of cedar. The Nortons have taken advantage of the beautiful lake view — the glass windows of their living room give a feeling of closeness to the out-of-doors. The use of natural materials and the openness to the exterior were characteristics of Frank Lloyd Wright houses. He and Henry Hobson Richardson were pioneer figures in the indigenous, modern American style.

The Morgans and Carnahans at 1507 and 1508 N. Lake Drive take advantage of the terrain. The houses are on different levels stepping down from the road to the lake. The Morgan house is in three sections with the larger section across the front.

The Japanese influence often found in "Contemporary" style is employed in the Aldredge cottage, 1523 N. Lake Drive. Enclosed at the rear of the house is a charming Japanese garden where visitors are welcome. On any Chautauquan's first visit to the grounds, this is truly a "must."

Recently built houses use the functional arrangement of Mr. Wright. All on one floor, the Howard Akin house at 32 Whittier commands a view of the out-of-doors and garden at the front, with bedrooms in the rear. Of natural wood, it blends in with the setting.

Chautauqua houses built after the turn of the century reflect the owners' individuality in style. They have a permanence about them. They tend to take advantage of the view and easy access to the out-of-doors as did those of the earliest cottage-holders.

The new institution buildings have a tendency to blend into the setting. This idea was paramount in Scott Lawson's mind in designing Bellinger Hall. The "contemporary" idea of functionalism follows the example of Frank Lloyd Wright.

Chris Norton, son of former President Ralph Norton, chose natural wood with many windows for his cottage at 1 Packard Manor.

Contemporary houses are larger, with many windows and enclosed areas so that they may be used as year-round homes. This one is at 1507 North Lake Drive.

Details borrowed from the Gothic (board and batten) show contemporary use of traditional ideas in this home at 1523 North Lake.

13

Color Harmony at Chautauqua

The use of color at Chautauqua has generally followed the ideas of Andrew Jackson Downing, the man who set the standards for cottage architecture in the nineteenth century.

Downing expressed the theory that the color of the house was the first impression seen by the eye. He emphasized the fact that we should avoid the colors nature avoids and copy those she offers, chiefly earth, stone, brick, and wood. Since houses are not built of foliage, they should not be painted green. He recommended Fawn, Drab, Gray stone, Brown stone, French gray, Slate sage, Straw, and Chocolate colors. The formula for mixing these colors is found in his book, *Cottage Residences*.[7] He felt that a cottage should be a mellow, cheerful shade and a mansion a graver color.

Mr. Downing really disliked white, which was the color used for most Greek Revival houses of the early nineteenth century. He thought the glare against green foliage made it unpleasant and recommended a color between cream and dust. The popular Chautauqua tan of the early cottages approximated this color. White was the most popular color for Classical buildings at the Chicago World's Fair, and it is presumed that Lewis Miller brought this idea back from the fair with him. The trim, Downing believed, should be painted a darker shade of the same color if the house were light and the reverse for a darkly painted house.

These were Downing's standards for harmony and beauty. The Victorians used many interesting combinations for contrasts. According to an early Chautauquan, these were often used on the grounds. The house at 34 Janes Avenue was originally gray with a bright red trim, and the one at 5 Thompson is still a popular early combination of white with pink.[8] How attractive two shades of green can be may be seen at 11 Morris Avenue. The architect of Bellinger Hall used earthy colors to blend the building into the area so that the overall picture of Chautauqua harmonizes with its natural surroundings.

I hope that the original colors of the houses found in Chautauqua's earlier period (South Avenue to Prospect) will be maintained and the remainder of the grounds be blended into the colors of nature. These colors may easily be found by scraping a little section of the structure if it hasn't completely peeled off. Chautauqua is a very special place, and it becomes more so with each return visit. We should all aim to keep it that way. It can remain special, in part, with an emphasis on perceptive harmonizing of colors.

14

Dr. and Mrs. Lucas still maintain the early
Chautauqua combination of white with
pink trim on their cottage at 5 Thompson.

Plans

Chautauqua cottages were planned for outdoor living. Housing facilities were mainly for sleeping and changing one's clothing. The religious and educational programs were paramount in the minds of Chautauquans. They prided themselves on near-perfect attendance.

Small vertical style cottages had living-rooms across the front and a lean-to or kitchen unit (many times of lattice) in the back. Often the main entrance was off the porch and led into the living room. A central stairway led to the second floor bedrooms. In the case of "guest" houses, a side door might lead to the second floor.

Even the Swiss Cottage of the Millers followed this plan originally. The living room was used as a sleeping room, and a stairway at the back led to the upstairs bedroom. The porch was used for entertaining, for everyone "stopped by" at 28 Miller Park upon disembarking from the boat.

By the 1890s there were boarding houses with three and four floors. The Ashland on Vincent is an example of this type of accommodation. Porches and windows were everywhere in evidence.

The 1900s brought more elaborate dwellings with as many as two living rooms. Architects were employed: Warren and Wetmore of New York for Packard Manor and Paul J. Pelz, architect of the Library of Congress, for the Hall of Christ. This was a complete reversal of direction from the days when cottage holders such as Erick Nelson of 26 Miller Avenue and the Reverend Mr. Foulke of 31 Janes built their own cottages.

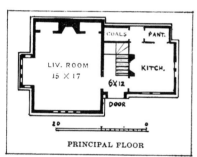

PRINCIPAL FLOOR

In many cottages the living room was on the front of the house, with an entrance into the hall, and the kitchen was on the right. In others, the living room was across the front with a side entrance to the upstairs bedrooms and the kitchen at the back.

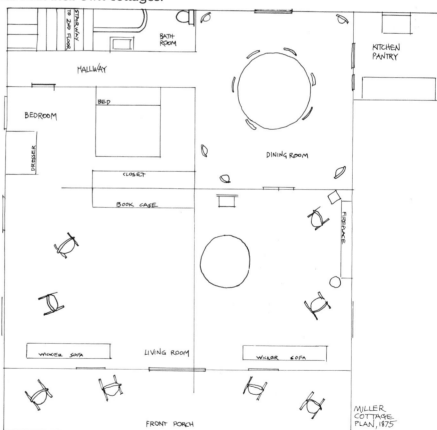

In the beginning Miller Cottage at 28 Miller Park was one large room with a bedroom on the second floor. Mina Miller Edison renovated it in 1922.

15

Materials

Since wood was plentiful in this area, most of the early buildings were constructed of this material. After midcentury, brick and brownstone were preferred by many Americans, and this was true in the case of Chautauquans. Wood was popular for houses. This practice was increased by the employment of wood in the "Eastlake Style." This attempt to mimic the furniture of this designer recognized the potential for decorative work and increased the use of the jigsaw and the lathe.

Using ready-made purchases from catalogues and stock plans, the builders freely combined different elements. Sears, Roebuck blueprints and stock doors and windows were used in building the home at 10 Bliss.

At the turn of the century more brick and stone were used in the buildings on the grounds. The Colonnade, Post Office, Refectory, Gate House, Smith Library, Packard Manor, and Lutheran House exhibit the use of these materials after 1900, indicating the move toward a permanent Chautauqua. Styles of the American colonies and the early Republic called for these substances, and, obviously, they added variety to the setting.

Where They Stayed

Even an "Ark" was represented by 1877 on Waugh and Summerfield Avenues with a boarding house described in the *Assembly Herald:* "Noah's Ark: why it should be given that classical name, I do not know. I thought, perhaps, it was on account of the animals harbored there. All the lions at Chautauqua were entertained at the Ark; all the monkeys, too, and once in a while we had a pig or so. I do not know but that is the reason that it was called the Ark. Afterward, it was called the 'Knowers Ark.' I think because there were so many people that knew so much that boarded there."[9]

On the ground floor lived the clear-voiced and musical Mr. Stephenson and his wife. College presidents were represented by Dr. Payne and George P. Hays, D.D., from Washington and Jefferson.

The Maynard family made one corner happy; Dr. Stephen Vail held classes in Hebrew in the portico. Professor J. Strong found sleeping accommodations on the lakeside. On the stairway might be found a notice not to throw water on the lower lodgers. Frank Beard lived like a typical artist near the roof. This chalker and talker refrained from covering the walls of the Ark with crayon and embellishments.

Professor William F. Sherwin, chiefly responsible for the musical programs of Chautauqua, left a rocking chair behind when he departed. Dr. Jesse L. Hurlbut, outstanding theologian and author, and Dr. Henry W. Warren, a noted clergyman, were also among the distinguished crew of the "Knowers Ark."

Built about 1875, celebrities were housed here at the Ark.

17

Hotel Athenaeum, built in 1881 at South Lake and Janes Avenue, boasted an additional tower.

The old Palace Hotel, 1874. Its location is now the site of the Athenaeum. In 1877 it served as the Post Office.

18

PALACE HOTEL

The Palace Hotel was located on a high bank above S. Lake Avenue between Janes and Simpson Avenue. It was built in 1877 from canvas covering used in the Philadelphia Centennial of 1876.

Three stories high, it was made of tent cloth over a wooden frame divided by muslin partitions. The snoring of some distinguished men could be heard by night since the partitions were far from soundproof. A good night's sleep was a rarity because cats congregated on the roof and held "concerts" and cat races.

ATHENAEUM HOTEL

The long porch covered the front of the building and commanded a beautiful view of the lake. The porch was lined with vacationers relaxing in wicker rockers of the type found on the grounds.

One of the towers has been removed from the top of the building. The Chautauqua Symphony Orchestra played on the porch on several Old First Night celebrations. The front lawn was always gay with lanterns, even in the rain!

Visitors arrived with baggage at the Palestine Avenue side of the building. There was a porch running the full length of this side also. Edward Weeks, John Ciardi, Karl Menninger, Jose Iturbi, Marian Anderson, Howard Mitchell, Arthur Fiedler, and Whittemore and Lowe are among the many distinguished guests of the Athenaeum.

One of the last surviving antebellum hotels, the Athenaeum retains its Victorian charm even with the top tower removed.

The main corridor of Hotel Athenaeum at Chautauqua looked like this in the early days.

Where They Met

PAVILION

A Pavilion, reached by a flight of wooden steps from Miller Park, was the meeting place in case of rain. Located at the North end of what is now the Plaza, it seated about 1,500 people.

The second Old First Night was held here in 1875. Heavy rain drove a large audience from the Auditorium in Miller Park to the Great Tabernacle on the Hill.

The tent which covered it was placed over the Amphitheater in the ravine from 1876 to 1878. The back of the ravine is on Clark Avenue between Bowman and Palestine Avenues.

The Auditorium that was used for a meeting place in the 1870s was a carry-over from the Camp Meeting. Gothic type cottages form the background.

In 1876 the Auditorium faced the lake and the seats were without backs. Chautauquans met under the trees for worship and programs.

The first Amphitheater was located in the natural ravine between Palestine and Bowman on Clark Avenue. The interior is a great example of the use of stick style.

20

The second Amphitheater, 1893.

AMPHITHEATER

It was a great step forward from the crude Auditorium and the tented Pavilion to the flat-roofed Amphitheater dedicated in 1879. Jesse L. Hurlbut, in his book *The Story of Chautauqua,* felt, however, that there was still room for improvement. He wrote: "But a heavy rain on the extensive roof would make even the largest-lunged orator inaudible...."[10]

The second Amphitheater was one story high with a steep roof that had to be shoveled in winter. It was supported by steel beams. The building, painted Chautauqua tan, was completed in 1893 and is still in use.

The surrounding area is well utilized to care for overflow crowds. There are accommodations for wheelchairs for the handicapped and earphones for the hard of hearing.

The present Amphitheater located between Clark and S. Terrace Avenues and Palestine and Bowman Avenues has the same uses as the original Auditorium located in Miller Park. It was the center of activity for religious services, lectures, music, and other entertainment.

Van Cliburn in performance.

The stage that is adjacent to the Athenaeum runs the full breadth of the Amphitheater. Behind it are a series of rooms for the convenience of program participants.

Many prominent people have been heard from this platform. President Franklin D. Roosevelt opened his 1936 campaign here with his "I Hate War" speech. Others who have been presented from this platform are Van Cliburn, the late Senator Robert F. Kennedy, Vice President Nelson A. Rockefeller, President Gerald Ford, Peter Nero, Marilyn Horne, Duke Ellington, Roberta Peters, and Eda LeShan.

HALL OF PHILOSOPHY

The original Hall of Philosophy was dedicated in 1879. It was styled after the Parthenon. Built in St. Paul's Grove, Dr. Vincent suggested the plan of the building. An open building, it was surrounded by plain columns that resembled marble but were made of wood.

Vesper services were held every Sunday afternoon at five o'clock. When Bishop Vincent and his family were in Europe, they always paused on Sunday to read the Chautauqua Vesper service.

In 1877, Mary A. Lathbury gave Chautauqua two songs that are cherished by countless Christians. "Day Is Dying in the West" and "Break Thou the Bread of Life" are still sung at Chautauqua, the former a traditional opening hymn for the Vespers and Song Service.

Mary Lathbury's immortal hymns were set to music by Professor William F. Sherwin, singer, chorus leader, Bible teacher, and wit.

The present building was completed in 1906. Mr. Albert Kelsey of Philadelphia was the architect. The building, encompassing a city block, is also located in the Grove. The roof is supported by 16 large columns of Doric style. They are made of cement and hold up the roof.

Later alterations include the construction of balustrades in 1925, and in 1965 the masonry and roof were renovated. This open-air theater is part of the unit of buildings that are used by the Chautauqua Literary and Scientific Circle. Lectures, vespers, and meetings are held here. Jane Addams, Edward Everett Hale, Dr. Howard Hanson, and Dr. Gösta Ehrensvärd, internationally recognized environmentalist-scientist, are among the many famous people who have spoken here.

On the Fletcher Avenue entrance the Golden Gate, through which the CLSC graduates pass each year, is to be found on the annual Recognition Day. Torchlights guided Chautauquans to this revered spot.

In the floor are inserted tablets in honor of the classes that contributed toward the building, and the CLSC parade is made meaningful by the participating classes marching behind their banners.

The first Hall of Philosophy built in 1879 at Clark and Cookman had pillars made of wood to resemble marble.

The present Hall of Philosophy built in 1906 expressed the founders' high regard for the classical.

The Golden Gate at Cookman and Fletcher is in place at the rear of the Hall of Philosophy on CLSC Recognition Day only. Dr. S. J. M. Eaton guards the gate through which the class will pass after completing the traditional graduation ceremony.

22

Where They Worshipped

The out-of-doors seemed to be the perfect place to worship in August of 1874. Auditorium, lakeside, and tents were used for the services.

In 1876, the Old Chapel was built on Clark and Miller Avenues. The residents on the grounds and the Assembly financed this building, which seated 200 people. It was built as a church for those who lived here year-round. This American Gothic structure was the first permanent public building erected at Chautauqua. According to Dr. Hurlbut, it was still standing in 1921.

Nearby, a Children's Temple was erected in 1878 on Miller between Pratt and Clark Avenues. Built through the largess of Lewis Miller, it was intended for a model Sunday School room. It consisted of a large central hall with platform and smaller rooms connected by folding doors.

Soon, many denominational buildings and the Amphitheater, Hall of Philosophy, and Hall of Christ would provide central meeting places for large groups of worshipers.

The Old Chapel built in 1876 on Clark and Miller Avenues was erected for a year-round church. An American Gothic structure, it was the first permanent public building in Chautauqua still standing in 1921.

Children's Temple was given in 1878 by Lewis Miller. Located across from the present Library site at Miller and Clark, it followed the plan of his Sunday School Hall in Akron, Ohio, a central assembly room with folding doors opening or closing a number of classrooms around it.

"Aula Christi" or Hall of Christ, at Wythe and South, was designed by Paul Pelz, architect of the Library of Congress.

An interior picture of the Hall of Christ taken at the rededication in July 1967. The renovation was made possible by Mrs. Robert Campbell and the Gebbie Foundation. My brother, Supreme Court Justice Rollin A. Fancher, is a member of the Executive Committee of this locally based philanthropic organization.

Where They Learned

Teaching through visual aids received a high priority at Chautauqua, and it was only natural that a museum played an important part from the beginning.

A large Museum Building was erected on the corner of Clark and Miller in 1882. This two story ediface boasted double doors and handsome bargeboard. Of Victorian style, the windows were long and narrow on the second floor and there were none on the first level. The interior was one large room with a balcony with stick style railings.

It shared the site with the CLSC Building. In 1890 the CLSC had new quarters in the building which housed the bookstore. Smith Library was built on the site in 1931.

The Museum collection was largely furnished by Lewis Miller. Among other things it contained 456 articles donated by the Egyptian Exploration Fund and the great panels of the Arch of Titus at Rome.

It was used as a museum until 1904 when it housed the School of Expression. The "Yearbook of 1895" gives an extensive account of the Museum's contents, but no one seems to know what happened to them. Included was an Egyptian mummy which was part of the collection!

This building at Clark and Miller was used as a museum until 1904 when it housed the School of Expression. The bargeboard under the eaves and the double doors are Victorian style characteristics.

The interior of the museum had a stick style railing on the second floor. It contained 456 articles donated by the Egyptian Exploration Fund, the great panels of the Arch of Titus at Rome, the Moabite Stone, and other items of varying importance.

The CLSC Class of 1963 maintains Pioneer Hall at Wythe at Cookman, built by the Class of 1882. Shown opening up the CLSC Museum are Helen Theurer, Mack Dill, and Louise Dill. The rest of the crew were Marian Neubauer, Julie Follansbee, Ruth Van Seventer, and Tony Van Seventer.

PIONEER HALL: 34 Cookman

Pioneer Hall at 34 Cookman was built by the first class to graduate from the CLSC. Located on the CLSC "quadrangle," it stands next to the Octagon House and across from the CLSC Alumni Hall and the Hall of Philosophy.

Built in 1885, it is of Gothic Revival style with a gable in front of a higher gable as a roof. The inside of the peaked roofs are filled with shingles of sawn art. There is an extension of the roof to the right of the gables.

A porch covers the front of the building with four steps leading up to the railed-in section. Spindle sawn art extends from left to right and is supported by columns with gingerbread in the corners. There are two rows of spindles below the roof.

Entrance is made into one large room through double doors with a transom of glass which reads "Pioneer Hall, 1885." On either side of the doors of this white clapboard building are windows. The hall serves as a museum for the CLSC. The artifacts on display include the pulpit used by Bishop John Vincent. The hall is lit only by candlelight and kerosene lamps.

This building is of historic value for two very specific reasons: first, because of its architectural uniqueness and secondly, because it played an important part in the early work of the CLSC, which initiated many far-reaching educational ideals in our nation. The CLSC began the idea for Continuing Education especially for those who could not attend colleges and universities.

The building is open for display after the CLSC meeting in the Hall of Philosophy and at special announced times. It has been recently renovated by the Class of 1963. They take charge of making it available to the public.

The Octagon Building, next to Pioneer Hall, was built for a classroom by the Pittsburgh members of the CLSC in 1885.

OCTAGON BUILDING

The Octagon Building, next to Pioneer Hall, was purchased by the classes of 1883 to 1886 in 1889. The Chautauqua *Assembly Herald* for August 15, 1885, announced: "Pittsburgh members of CLSC built a dainty little octagon cottage."

As early as 1804, Thomas Jefferson had erected an octagonal building on his farm. Several eight-sided buildings may be found in western New York. Happily, one found its way to the Chautauqua Grounds.

Located on the corner of Wythe and Cookman, the building is composed of a small sized room with long narrow windows. Poetry classes for the Creative Writer's Workshop have been held here by such eminent poets as Robert Francis, John Ciardi, and John Holmes.

This small white clapboard building has Gothic peaks on all sides. There is a hood over the door with elaborate carved brackets supporting it. This charming building adds variety to the Victorian buildings on the grounds.

25

Where They Learned

The alumni of the Normal Classes for Sunday School Teachers showed their gratitude to Chautauqua by building Normal Hall in 1885. Classes had been originally held in tents near the Auditorium in Miller Park.

The original building located at Pratt and Scott Avenues had a Greek Revival quality with a small portico entrance on Scott Avenue. A pillared porch stretched along the Pratt Avenue side with decorative sawn art in the overhanging gables.

In 1914, an addition was built. The Music Department made use of the building, and later it was transferred to the Summer Schools. Located next to Norton Hall, it was taken over as a facility for the Performing Arts.

In the 1960s, Normal Hall was used as a practice studio for the Opera Company, and the space is now used by them for building scenery.

The Moorish Barn, built in 1887 on College Hill Park, was the home of Chautauqua's degree-giving university. It was razed in 1919. The Arts and Crafts Buildings replaced it.

A handsome piece of sawn art made by Frank Fox, who built and decorated the original Normal Hall. A gift of the alumni of the Normal Class of Sunday School Teachers, the building had a Greek Revival quality.

CHAUTAUQUA COLLEGE OF LIBERAL ARTS

In 1887, a College of Liberal Arts was built high upon College Hill overlooking the lake on Wythe at Harris and Prospect. William Rainey Harper, who came to Chautauqua in 1883 as instructor in the School of Languages, was its head.

The educational programs of Chautauqua had increased by the proverbial "leaps and bounds," bearing out its second purpose of "education" announced on the sign by the Gate, "The Place where Religion, Education and Recreation Meet."

In 1885, a charter was granted by the State of New York incorporating the Chautauqua University. In 1886, the Department of Physical Education was inaugurated under the direction of Dr. W. G. Anderson of the Adelphi Academy in Brooklyn. Thus began the first summer schools in the United States.

It was time to incorporate the educational programs into a more coordinated area. Tents, small buildings, and temporary quarters had served their purpose. A College of Liberal Arts Building was begun.

The Moorish porticos and domes, like something out of *Arabian Nights,* have been credited with the building being called "The Moorish Barn." The front was decorated with horseshoe and crescent arches and delicate traceries. The Moorish influence in architecture might be seen on the Athenaeum as well as buildings in Saratoga Springs, New York, during this period. The college building housed a permanent library of about 1,500 volumes and a chemical laboratory.

George Vincent and William Rainey Harper contributed greatly to the success of the college. Many of the ideas they helped to put into practice at Chautauqua were used in the posts they assumed later.

Dr. Harper became President of the University of Chicago in 1895. Yet he continued to supervise the work at the college at Chautauqua. George Vincent served as President of the University of Minnesota beginning in 1911 and later as President of the Rockefeller Foundation. Dr. Harper put his experiences with summer study, university extension, and correspondence to good use at Chicago, and George Vincent reorganized extension work at Minnesota.

The college building stood until 1919 and was then torn down.

KELLOGG HALL

Women have always played an important part in Chautauqua's activities and contributions. Kellogg Hall is a building dedicated to a woman who was a devoted Chautauquan and who provided facilities for activities of special interest to women.

In an article in the *Tribune Monthly Herald* for September, 1890, the activities carried on in the building are described in this manner:

Coeducation is one of the admirable features of the Chautauqua plan. Women are in the ascendant and take a leading part in all the exercises. Wherever you turn you meet them – applauding at piano recitals, taking notes at lectures on Dante, digging up Greek roots at the college, reading "Le Gendre de M. Poirier" in the original, discussing the Hebrew prophets with Dr. Harper, seated before an easel under the trees, splashing about in the lake, or girt with an apron and compounding pie-crust in the cooking tent.

Anne Kellogg Memorial Hall was erected on Vincent Avenue on the site of the present Colonnade. James H. Kellogg, a wealthy merchant of Troy, New York, erected the building in memory of his mother, a devoted Chautauquan.

Dedicated in 1889, it is of Romanesque style.[11] Its pointed towers are conspicuous objects on the grounds. Mr. Calkins was the architect. Elaborate ornamentation is found on the front along with distinctive pillars. The tower on the left boasts a graceful stairway that gives a lift to the spirit.

27

Kellogg Hall at Pratt and Ramble was moved from Vincent to provide more room for a playground for the kindergarten.

Part of the first floor of Kellogg Hall was for the use of the W.C.T.U. Miss Frances Willard, in a letter of October 9, 1876, to Bishop Vincent reminds him: "Our National had its inception at Chautauqua you remember."[12] On July 22, 1904, Mr. and Mrs. John C. Martin presented a window to Kellogg Hall in Miss Willard's memory. Mr. Martin, in making the presentation, said: "No one who has spoken on the Chautauqua platform received such ovations as were given to her." Miss Willard was one of the first women to speak before the Assembly. In 1925, the window was moved to 32 S. Lake—the new W.C.T.U. Headquarters. Later, in 1948, it was moved to the group's national headquarters in Evanston, Illinois.

The *Tribune Monthly* comments that the Anne M. Kellogg Memorial Building provides rooms for five departments of women's work. The kindergarten and normal classes shared the first floor with the W.C.T.U. A school of wood carving, a drawing department, and a school of cooking and Delsarte classes complete the early opportunities offered.

The building was moved to Ramble and Pratt Avenues in 1905 to make way for the Colonnade and to have more room for children to play. Presently, Kellogg Hall houses the summer schools offices.

ALUMNI HALL: Wythe Avenue (between South and Cookman)

Alumni Hall is the home of the Chautauqua Literary and Scientific Circle—the oldest book club in America. Of Victorian style, it was built in 1892 by the CLSC classes with Mr. E. G. Hall of Syracuse, New York, as the architect and Mr. E. G. Lepar of Jamestown, New York, as the builder.

A Chautauqua Institution building, it forms a nucleus with Pioneer Hall (the CLSC Museum), the Octagon House (formerly used for creative writing classes in poetry), and the Hall of Philosophy (where its meetings are held).

The main "Club" building of the CLSC, it houses the class banners (over 90). The banners, which show the mottos of each year's class, have been carried each year in the Recognition Day parade, the day of "graduation" of members who have completed the initial four years of reading. Many of the banners are very beautiful and of historic interest.

Noteworthy are the panelled friezes around the building. The large porch has Doric columns holding up its roof. The Sandwich

Alumni Hall at Wythe and Cookman is the main building of the CLSC. Social gatherings and classes are held in this Victorian building with classical touches.

Poets, a group who enjoy their sandwiches before a session of critiqueing each other's poems, meet weekly on this porch during the season. A three-sided, third floor porch is decorated with columns and is based on a second floor bay. Two cupola windows permit natural light on the third floor.

At the opening of the 1891 season, CLSC numbered more than a 100,000 members. The classes enjoyed meeting together and its eight classrooms were furnished by the gifts received from members. The large hall on the second floor was used on Recognition Day by the graduating class. After Kate F. Kimball's death in 1917, it was named "The Kimball Room."

Kate Kimball holds a special place in the hearts of CLSC members. When Dr. Vincent interviewed her for the position of Secretary of the CLSC at age 18, he said: "I am afraid that you are too young to undertake this work." She convinced him to let her try. She proved invaluable. Jesse Hurlbut writes: "Next to the originating genius of John H. Vincent, the influence which made the Chautauqua Home Reading Course one of the mightiest educational forces of the nineteenth century was the tireless energy and executive ability of Kate F. Kimball."[13] Frank Chapin Bray, editor of *The Chautauqua Magazine,* called her "a kind of Chautauqua Mother Superior."

In recent years the building has been used for creative writing classes as well as CLSC gatherings. Several interested members are working on refurbishing the building, and it is hoped that it will resume its former role as a social and educational center for its Centennial in 1978.

Some Chautauquans joke that CLSC means "Come, Love, Sit Closer!" Dr. Edwin P. Booth, in his CLSC Recognition Day Address in the Amphitheater in 1966, enlarged the meaning to "Come love, sit closer to humanity. Come love, sit closer to art. Come love, sit closer to music. Come love, sit closer to literature. Come love, sit closer to sociology. Come love, sit closer to all the great minds, voices, melodies, dreams, ideas of the past." He then closed with: "Come Love, sit closer to all these mighty dreams!"[14]

Hall of Education, formerly the Hall of Pedagogy, may be called "eclectic" architecture since it borrows from the Classical and Victorian. It is on Wythe Avenue between Hurst and Harris.

HALL OF EDUCATION

The Hall of Education, a vital center of Chautauqua's educational system, was erected as the Hall of Pedagogy on College Hill in 1898. Chautauqua, first in the field of summer schools, was still leading in attendance. John H. Vincent laid the cornerstone for summer schools at Chautauqua and subsequently for America. In due time they became as characteristically American and widespread as the American skyline.

The building was moved from Pratt facing Harris to Wythe between Hurst and Harris Avenues in 1911. The architecture of the Hall of Education may be called "eclectic" since it borrows from several styles. The pillars rising two stories form the center of interest and carry out the Classical mode of many Chautauqua buildings. The gabled roof covers the turrets on each end of this brown shingled building.

29

Where They Shopped
and Conducted Business

Business was first conducted from tents and Camp Meeting dwellings. On August 17, 1889, fire destroyed some of these buildings located on the southwest side of Miller Park in the area where the Arcade now stands, including the site of the first local Fire Department. Until the coming of the Chautauqua Traction in 1917, this was the main business district of Chautauqua. It then moved up the hill to what is now Bestor Plaza. An old business block and Post Office flourished on the south side of Vincent Avenue when it extended through the present plaza.

COLONNADE

In 1905, the Colonnade Building was built to house the stores and institution business offices. Built on the present site, it was destroyed by fire in 1907. The contents of the stores and much of the institution's printed matter were destroyed.

It was immediately rebuilt with stately classical columns and a walkway entrance. It was of red brick with white trim, and the third story contained apartments.

Again in 1961, fire swept through the Colonnade, completely destroying the third floor, which was never rebuilt. The institution offices moved to the second floor of Smith Library. By the following season the Colonnade was again ready for occupancy by the administrative staff.

President William J. Carothers was largely responsible for the completion of the new Colonnade. The outside of the building remains the same and presents an impressive sight when looking across Bestor Plaza.

This stick style building at Vincent near Ames served as a Post Office.

The Post Office built in 1909 on Clark between Vincent and Miller has a Classical Revival quality. Two-story columns impart a stately quality to this brick with white trim building—the center for local news.

Stores faced Vincent Avenue, which continued through what is now Bestor Plaza. These buildings were destroyed by fire in 1904.

The neo-classical Colonnade incorporated stores and institution business offices on Bestor Plaza in 1905. The nostalgic Pergola is the vine-covered refreshment stand in front of the Colonnade.

31

The Colonnade Milk Bar on Ames Avenue sold this favorite drink in 1905.

A second Colonnade replaced the first except that the third story was never restored after a fire in 1961.

Welch Pavilion,

How They Lived

The architecture of the houses carried over from the Sunday School Assembly was primitive. Some of the cottages on Miller Park stand on the same spot as the ones illustrated in the pictures. Parts of the wooden buildings have been incorporated into some of the present houses.

Even at this early date it is obvious that easy access to the out-of-doors was the distinctive characteristic of Chautauqua architecture. Houses were characterized by peaked roofs and vertical board and batten construction. The early lots were very narrow and led to long narrow buildings. Lattice and vines gave privacy to the cottages built closely together. Cottage owners stepped onto the ground or onto small porches in 1874.

There were 12 streets and 135 cottages in 1874 when the First Assembly was held.[15]

THE SECOND ASSEMBLY

The Second Assembly heralded the completion of the Miller Cottage in time for President Grant's visit in 1875.

THE THIRD ASSEMBLY

The success of the Assembly was shown by the extension of the season to 24 days in 1876.

Fortunately, the *Chautauqua Daily Assembly Herald* listed the cottage owners at Fair Point in their July 27, 1876 issue. It follows.

Vol. I – Chautauqua Daily Assembly Herald – July 27, 1876
Second issue – Page 3 – column 2

Cottage Owners at Fair Point
The following is a list, nearly complete, of the persons owning owning cottages at the Point this evening. It is accurate as it was possible to make under the circumstances:

AUDITORIUM	ASBURY AVE.	NORTH AVE.	TERRACE AVE.	SUMMERFIELD AVE.	ROBERTS AVE.
Dr. Vincent	W. S. Wealey	Rev. E. J. L. Baker	C. R. Johnson & Co.	(all burned in 1887)	Thomas Park
Lewis Miller	S. S. Paddock	E. Eaton	Lawton & Prossner	Charles Payne	Rev. O. L. Mead
Post Office	Rev. J. E. Chapin	N. Felton	W. O. Brownell	Mrs. Archibald	Cuenny & Harp
Bromagim	Rev. J. W. Staples	Mrs. Leslie	S. W. Baujean	S. S. Burbon & Co.	
L. Fullager	Office of Superintendant	Rev. R. W. Scott	Fred Taylor	Hatch & Johnson	HEDDING AVE.
R. M. Harper	of Grounds	Dr. Smith	Rev. A. Losee	Miner Curtis G.	Thomas Morris
W. S. Ecker	M. M. McCullough	W. S. Gleason	P. W. Bemis	W. Kluck	Sinby & Hutson
Mrs. H. Barber	Cornell Brothers	Mrs. Stevens	C. P. Davis	Mrs. Hurlbut	Hewes & Son
Office of Pres. of	Rev. J. H. Starrett	Mrs. Stewart	O. Wagoner	Rev. A. H. Bowers	O. J. Green & Co.
Grounds	N. B. Dunham	Davis & Company	W. N. Reno	Guests lodging	J. W. Pitts & Co.
Editorial Rms. CAH	Section Tent D	J. B. Murry	Beck & Wilson	Rooms, E. L. Alling	Kinnear & Brayton
Section Tent A, B, & C	Rev. Chesbro & Co.	Curtis & Skiff	Mrs. E. C. Smith		A. M. Kelsey
Rev. R. M. Warren	E. Greely	A. N. Craft	Mrs. Bundy	MORRIS AVE.	Fred Badcock
Rev. Joseph Leslie	Fire Department		Scofield & Hurlbut	Rev. A. C. Tibbets	J. W. Harmon
Rev. W. H. Mooseman	C. P. Davis	WHITFIELD AVE.	Rev. D. M. Stever	H. K. VanRenselaer	John Black
J. B. Fischer & Co.	Mrs. Sarah Burnell	O. Bond	Miss Loosie	H. Harmon	M. Bloomer
Rev. W. H. Wilson	Mr. P. Holmes	Filmore Klock	Cyrus Woodard	Rev. Norton	A. W. Billing
Rev. H. H. Moore	Rev. T. B. Warren	Dr. Curtis	N. F. Wilson	W. A. Selkregg	H. Palmer
Rev. M. Smith Jones	E. S. Norbon	S. Evans	Dawson	J. B. Compton	William Keeler
Bowkens & Co.	Rev. L. W. Shadduck	F. E. Miller	M. Dewey	Mrs. Martha Mitchell	
Rev. J. E. Chapin	Kerland & Young	Mrs. C. Ransom	Gallup & Hinkley	E. J. Simons	SIMPSON AVE.
Rev. F. A. Archibald	Hardenburg & Company	Dr. W. Ransom	Dana Horton	Lorenzo Martin	Rev. Wiliam Rice
Mrs. Susan Ma Ross	F. D. Kennedy	M. A. Martin	Shiram Harker	A. C. Light	Rev. J. E. Chapin
C. L. Jeffords	Rev. J. Garnett	Mrs. Maltby	G. Flaggler	Rev. Squire	Nelson
W. D. Hatch	C. Showell	Milton Bailey	H. A. Ebersoll	and Seely	P. W. Scofield
Moffet & Mead	C. S. Johnson	Business Office Sunday	H. W. Sperry	Pavilion	Mrs. Rodgers
M. E. Society	Oriental House	School – Association Herald	R. F. Stockeg		T. B. Green
Sherman	Phelps & Stewart		Samuel Wilcox		Hiram A. Pratt
N. Y. R. R.	E. B. Hobart				Rev. H. A. Lindley
Rev. E. J. L. Baker	Klock Pickard & Company				H. P. Mallick
D. R. Baker	R. E. Brown				Rev. T. Brown
J. M. Seymour	Branch & Bently				Rev. R. W. Carley
Sardis Stewart	Mrs. Kluck, Hunt, Windsor,				William Scofield
	& Palmeter				C. D. Colburn
	Mrs. James Patterson				Charles Salisbury
					S. H. Jones
					J. E. Chapin
					Rev. M. Bennet

14 Miller Park (Lot 23)

This property was first leased to Sardius Steward, of Panama, New York, the largest farm owner of the county. Mr. Steward of Ashville, New York, had 1,300 acres in dairy farms. Floyd Darrow wrote of his father in 1953: "It is a matter of family pride that the first wooden cottage to be erected at Chautauqua, then called Fairpoint, was built by Mr. Steward. It is still standing in Miller Park." Mr. Sardius Steward leased the land in 1873.

This Gothic Revival house, listed in the Chautauqua *Assembly Herald* of 1876, was built before 1876. Of medium gray, it has a porch with columns and stick railings across the front. A brick chimney was built on the left side of the house. The porch has a flat roof and the sides of the roof of this house were turreted and lead to a peak. There are two windows on the second story front with green blinds. There is an addition on the back of the house.

The cottage is located on the corner of Thompson Street and Miller Park next to the John Paul Jones cottage. It was indexed in the Directory under Mrs. Alfred Wicks' name as early as 1903. Sara Wick Dale is the present owner.

26 S. Terrace

The house at 26 S. Terrace is one of the oldest houses, if not the oldest house, on the Institution Grounds. The earliest lease is dated 1873, but the owner believes it was probably built before then. The lease was granted by the Sunday School Assembly. Miss Wilma E. Lander, the owner, has in her possession a letter stating that it was always in the family Blodgett and that it was built on the present site some years before Chautauqua was founded.

Blodgett, a carpenter, built the house, installing hand-built cupboards and a secretary, among other things, which are still being used. The house has ginger-bread and is of Carpenter Gothic architecture. Built of clapboard on the front and sides, it has board and batten at the rear. Like many Terrace Avenue houses it is built on an embankment with stairs with iron railings leading up to the lower porch. The lake and Amphitheater are easily accessible from this residence.

26 S. Terrace (second from left) is probably the oldest house on the grounds. The owner has proof that the Blodgett family built it on the present site before the Assembly was founded.

Many repairs and alterations have been made. It has had a new foundation, roof, and the first and second story porches have also been rebuilt. The rear doors have been rebuilt and some windows have been replaced. The floors have been secured by new stringers. Even though the kitchen has been remodeled, it still retains its old early Chautauqua character.

Efforts have been made to winterize the white painted house by lining the rooms and modernizing the bath. There is a garden both in the front and in the back of the house. The house is in close proximity to its neighbors.

33

20 Center

Booker T. Washington stayed in this cottage when he spoke at Chautauqua in 1896. Formerly a rooming house, the cottage is now used by the Pipers as a family dwelling with an apartment which they rent.

The house is one of a whole row of typical Victorian cottages with open porches and doors. The roof goes up to a Gothic peak and it has gingerbread trim. The upper porch has a railing made of sawn art. There are two doors on each porch which give easy access to the out-of-doors.

Built in 1875, this house is located very near to Bestor Plaza. In 1881, the *Chautauqua Assembly Herald* of July 30 lists Mrs. W. Ward as owner. It is presently owned by Mr. and Mrs. Warren Piper of California, Pennsylvania.

28 Miller Park, Lewis Miller Cottage

Lewis Miller Cottage, home of Chautauqua's co-founder Lewis Miller, is the only National Landmark in Chautauqua County. It is also the first precut house in America still standing. Mr. Miller, prominent Akron industrialist and educator, had it cut in Akron and brought to Chautauqua in 1875.

The cottage is located on a knoll at 28 Miller Park and overlooks the site of the original Auditorium and the lake. It was one of the early centers of hospitality and was erected in time for President Ulysses Grant's visit in 1875.

The house is of "Swiss Cottage" style with structural crisscross frame on the exterior. The original house had a striped tent to the right side for a men's dormitory, although some members of the Miller family intimate that President Grant slept upstairs on the second floor. There is still a washstand that he is said to have used.

The second floor of the Cottage was a dormitory for ladies. Lewis and Mrs. Miller slept in a folding bed that had a mirror at one end when folded up. This was kept at the left rear of the front living room.

There was a stairway behind the folding bed to the second floor. A cabinet at the back of the room housed the kitchen facilities, since the Millers ate at the Athenaeum or the nearby boarding house except for a light breakfast, tea, or punch.

Mina Miller, daughter of Lewis Miller, married Thomas Edison in their Oak Place home in Akron. Many changes were effected after she became the owner of the Miller Cottage. She installed the kitchen wing and bedroom, made a second story wing, redesigned the interior, and laid out a beautiful garden in the back of the Chautauqua cottage. The downstairs bedroom was used by the Edisons.

After President Grant's visit, the Henry Fords, Lowell Thomas, and Adolph Ochs were among those supplementing the guest list.

Charles Edison, Edison's son, former Governor of New Jersey, and Secretary of the Navy under Franklin D. Roosevelt in 1939 and 1940, was present at the ceremony in 1966 when the cottage became a National Landmark.

Margaret Miller Newman, a grand daughter of Lewis Miller, remembers watermelon parties on the porch. The house, owned since 1951 by Nancy Arnn, Mina Edison's niece, is maintained by Nancy and her young family in true preservationist style.

Booker T. Washington stayed in this American Gothic guest house at 20 Center when he spoke here.

Miller's inventions greatly affected the life-style of the family at 28 Miller Park.

The hundredth birthday of Lewis Miller and the fiftieth year of the invention of the light bulb by Thomas Edison was celebrated in front of the Miller Cottage with fireworks and bright lights. Elmer E. Fancher, a student at the University of Cincinnati and the Niagara Power Company, was in charge of the lighting display and the building of the new substation.

Several houses were torn down to make a garden for the Miller Cottage. Elaborate stick motifs were attached to the sides.

On July 6, 1966, John A. Carver, Under-secretary of the Department of Interior, presented a plaque designating Miller Cottage as a National Landmark to Dr. Curtis Haug, President of Chautauqua Institution.

Mr. and Mrs. Thomas A. Edison in their garden behind the Miller Cottage. Mrs. Edison was the daughter of Lewis Miller. After her marriage to Edison they summered here.

The offices of the Chautauqua *Assembly Herald* in 1882 at 5 Whitfield were later transformed into two apartments.

5 Whitfield Avenue
Fairpoint Cottage

This Gothic Revival cottage was the new office of the *Assembly Herald,* Chautauqua's first newspaper, in 1876. Theodore Flood, later in charge of *The Chautauquan,* was the editor.

Built just off Miller Park, it is the third house to the right of the Miller Cottage. When it was built circa 1873 it began as a tent platform. Now it consists of two completely separate apartments that are made adjoining by inside doors.

Fairpoint Cottage has undergone many alterations since it was originally built. In 1974, the gingerbread was restored and the cottage looks almost exactly like it did in 1876. The interior doors date from 1889 when it was a boarding house. Plank seat chairs, presently in the house, date back to at least 1889.

The house was transferred to Joseph O. Patton, Jr., in 1973. It is used in the summer by his children and their families. "What interesting tales the repairing carpenter could tell," the Pattons reflect.

36

In 1975 the gingerbread was restored on the Gothic Revival cottage at 5 Whitfield.

12 Miller Park
The Tionesta

This Gothic Revival cottage with its porches and peaked gable is typical of early Chautauqua cottages. The lot was owned by A. M. Warren in 1873. Leased by C. L. Jeffords in 1874, we find him listed in the "Persons Owning Cottages on the Point" in the Chautauqua *Assembly Herald* of July 27, 1876.

The house is of Chautauqua tan clapboard with dark brown trim. The porches across the front have railings with narrow posts. A delicate piece of sawn art and a finial in the peak are visible to the viewer. A window in the front has colored glass squares in the side and upper border.

In 1903, we find Miss Emma Rose Howard listed in the Directory. She left the house to the Dithridge sisters. The present owner's mother, Ethelyn Dithridge Hotaling, was a poet.

The house may be called a place where the muses gathered since she entertained the Chautauqua Winter Poetry Circle in her home. Several of her poems were included in *Tapestry,* which was published by the Circle. Her daughter, Rachel Hermann, has placed first in the Chautauqua Woman's Club Poetry Contest.

The house is built on a typical narrow lot, as are most of the houses on Miller Park, with a cottage owned by the Robert Wilders of New York City on the right and one owned by Sarah Wick Dale of Butler, Pennsylvania on the left.

20 Miller Park
Alfred M. Landon Home

The name Alfred M. Landon Home gives us the clue to its claim to fame. It was built by the Rev. W. H. Mossman, grandfather of Alfred Mossman Landon, the nominee for the presidency of the United States against Roosevelt in 1936. Landon met his first wife here. She was a neighbor in the house across the street which is still standing at 22 Miller Park. The Landon's daughter, Peggy, was a fourth generation Chautauquan. Landon spoke at Chautauqua in 1936.

One of the most attractive cottages on the grounds, 20 Miller Park faces the place where the first Auditorium was located and where Chautauqua had its beginnings. The early houses on Miller Park were built closely together and most of them date from 1876. Of typical cottage style, the house was built by the Rev. Mossman in 1876.

It begins a row of cottages having Gothic Revival characteristics. The roof goes up to a peak with long narrow windows and doors. There is a lovely bay on the Whitfield Avenue side, a Queen Anne characteristic, which lets sunlight into the living room across the front of the house. It is of earthy gray color trimmed with pink.

Alf Landon, presidential nominee in 1936, spent his summers at 20 Miller Park with his grandfather, Rev. W. H. Mossman.

There are two porches which give easy access to the out-of-doors. The exterior was slightly altered in 1937 when the back porch was enclosed to expand the kitchen and make room for a downstairs bathroom. The second floor was expanded earlier for an upstairs bathroom. The front porch entrance leads into the living room, and behind that is a dining room with a stairway leading to three upstairs bedrooms.

In 1914, Mr. E. H. Overton purchased the house. He sold it in 1919 to Mrs. Louise Sumner and later in 1961 Mrs. Ann M. MacMillan bought it.

The inside is of wainscoting. It has not been altered but is painted pink. Much of the original furniture still remains and is stamped with the name of the first owners and builders. Several of the original prints and pictures still hang on the walls.

30 Miller Park (Lot 49)
(1 S. Terrace)

Thomas Edison stayed at 30 Miller Park when he was courting Mina Miller prior to their marriage on February 24, 1886. He taught her the Morse Code on the lake by tapping on her hand. Later, he proposed in Morse Code and she tapped, "yes." Known as the Alling for many years, it was one of the best hostelries.

The house is a three story gray Victorian building with an entrance facing Simpson Avenue. Gay red rockers brighten the long porches. The cottage overlooks Chautauqua Lake and Miller Park with an open lot in the front.

The leases go back to the Rev. J. H. Starrett in 1873. He is listed as a cottage owner in 1876. The cottage was leased to Mrs. E. A. Alling of Akron, Ohio in 1890.

In 1901, it was listed under the name of John R. Connor of Franklin, Pennsylvania, and was renovated in 1903 at a cost of $3,000 according to the Chautauqua *Assembly Herald* of July 7, 1903. In 1947, it became the property of Chautauqua Institution.

Since 1962 it has been owned by Milton M. Ronsheim of Cadiz, Ohio, and Andrew W. Miller of Steubensville, Pennsylvania.

Mr. Ronsheim is the Co-Publisher and Editor of the *Harrison News-Herald,* and Mrs. Ronsheim is the Director of the Chautauqua Literary and Scientific Circle. In 1974, he was the first journalist to volunteer for the Volunteer in Mission. The Ronsheims spent three to four months visiting church schools and hospitals in northern India. Mr. Miller is a lawyer.

16 N. Terrace, 11 Whitfield
Chautauqua Inn
Eau Clair and Annex
Beaujean Boarding Cottage

Mr. Sanford Beajean, who built the old Beaujean Boarding Cottage in 1876, was also the architect. The present Chautauqua Inn has an entrance on 16 N. Terrace and 11 Whitfield Avenue.

The Inn is only one block away from the Miller Cottage. It has three floors topped by a mansard roof. There are open porches on both streets. It is constructed of clapboard with interlocking joints. The porches have railings with spindles and posts. There are gingerbread decorations on the porches of this Victorian style dwelling. In recent years the interior has been remodeled to include a sprinkler system and more up-to-date plumbing.

In addition to being a carpenter, Mr. Beaujean was a cobbler and had his shoe repair shop in the building next to the Boarding Cottage. He allowed people to use his special well water for 25¢ per week. No. 14 and 16 N. Terrace were connected by a walking bridge. Mr. Sanford Beaujean owned both of these cottages and also 13 Whitfield.

Mr. Beaujean was Mrs. W. M. Gibbs' uncle by marriage to her father's sister. Mr. and Mrs. Gibbs ran the Inn for many years as the Eau Claire and Annex. Walter M. Gibbs was the author of *Spices and How to Know Them.*

Bernice Lampher, the present onwer, bought the Inn from Gibbs' daughter Clara, a retired art teacher. Once a year, Ms. Lampher has a musicale with a guest artist. This custom was begun by Mrs. W. M. Gibbs, a piano teacher.

One of the more famous musicales featured Paul Scharnfield, who has played under Bernstein on national television. While studying with the noted concert pianist and teacher, Ozan Marsh, Paul resided at the Inn.

Jane Nelson, Chautauqua artist, has captured the charm of this Victorian cottage at 16 N. Terrace. Sanford Beaujean, who built this boarding house, was also its architect.

How They Lived (1877-1881)

After 1876, more houses were built in the Miller Park area. Many were built up Vincent and Miller with branch settlements to the north and south. The ones in the central area were "cottage style," predominantly Gothic, and were built on small lots.

A few elaborate homes such as 2 Roberts and 1 Morris Avenues dotted the landscape. A hotel and restaurant were located in this central area. In 1877, we also find the "Old Chapel," the first permanent building, being used. That same year, Fair Point became Chautauqua by enactment of the legislature.

The beginning of the Chautauqua Scientific and Literary Circle was the highlight of the year 1878. The Children's Temple, given by Lewis Miller, was dedicated in that same year. It was located on Miller Avenue across from Smith Library.

The year 1879 revealed the completion of the first Amphitheater and the first Hall of Philosophy.

26 N. Terrace

One of the first cottages built near the junction of Terrace and Morris Avenues was 26 N. Terrace. Erected in 1877, the first owner was the Hon. Albert Dow, U.S. Senator from Jamestown, New York. He sold it to Mrs. Spencer Ward.

Dr. Spencer Ward emigrated from Vermont and his hobby was sheep raising. His wife, Helen Ward, was the largest landowner in Chautauqua County, according to her granddaughter, Marion Thomas.[16] The Wards' daughter, Harriet, was the wife of Frederick W. Thomas, Editor of the *Silver Creek Gazette* and a pioneer in the insurance business. Miss Marion Thomas came to her grandparents' cottage in 1892 when she was four years old. She now resides at the St. Elmo Hotel.

One side of the house overlooks the Campbell Garden. John Vincent kept his boat on the lot until later when Mr. Reed built a house on it. This house, 25 Whitfield, is the home of C. Campbell Putnam.

Of American Gothic style, the roof of 24 N. Terrace goes up to a peak with unadorned bargeboard. The upstairs porch has a sawn ornament railing. The lower floor porch has been recently installed and the supports are plain. The front porch has been shingled. The original clapboard of this dwelling remains. This cottage is painted yellow with green trim. It was originally white with green sashes.

The door to the left of the porch leads into the front sitting room. At the right end of the porch is a door into a hall with a stairway leading to the second floor bedrooms. In back of the front room is a dining room, kitchen, and pantry. There was no roof over the porch originally but later it was covered to make a place to play on rainy days.

The house is now owned by Mrs. G. L. Eberhack, great-granddaughter of the Wards. The family have preserved both the interior and exterior in early Chautauqua style.

32 Miller Park

Archibald D. and Abbie Falconer, descendants of the family which founded Falconer, New York, were pioneer residents at 32 Miller Park. In 1903 it is listed under the name of Helen Falconer.[17] Dr. Frank M. Falconer and his sister, Katherine, became the owners in 1951. Today, Dr. Falconer's widow summers here.

Albert M. Catlin of Sinclair-ville held the lease in 1877. In the Chautauqua Assembly and University list of properties for rent in 1888, we find a listing under 48 Asbury (now 32 Miller Park) by him. Listed in 1876, it was built on a tent platform.

The cottage is sandwiched in between 30 and the Albion at 55 Terrace and overlooks the lake. It has been designated as Eclectic architecture since it combines the best of several styles. It has stick style railings on the second floor porch and vertical lines of Gothic Revival and Classical columns of Greek Revival. It has porches on two levels and the exterior is white clapboard.

Ernest LaPrade, author of *Alice in Orchestralia,* a popular book published for children, lived in the ground floor apartment when he studied music at Chautauqua.

6 Vincent Avenue

Captain P. W. Bemus, Chief of the Chautauqua Police, built this cottage in 1877. Sandwiched in between the Sunny Veranda and the Constant-Fix-Inn, it has porches on both the first and second levels.

Of Gothic Revival style, it boasts a peaked roof. The porches are held up by columns. An unusual detail is the use of shingles as a porch railing. Built on a slant, it has a cement basement. There are many windows on the porches which provide a view of the lake.

Captain Bemus is remembered for the Frank Beard caricature in the Chautauqua *Assembly Herald* of July 13, 1899. He is pictured on his bicycle with his long beard flying, as Police Chief at the turn of the century. In 1877 the police numbered 60 men.[18] A native of Bemus Point, Bemus also served in the Civil War.

The present owners of the house are L. Fulton and Roger Clouse. Mr. Clouse is a former Chautauqua Trustee and a prominent Cleveland banker.

40

Thirty-two Miller Park, which commands one of the finest views of Miller Park, was the summer home of the descendants of the family that founded Falconer, New York.

The Genial Protector of the Public Safety.

Civil War Captain Philander W. Bemus, Chief of Police at the turn of the century, is caricatured. Bemus built the house at 6 Vincent.

14 Cookman (Lot 527)

The Chautauqua tradition of fine entertainment was carried on by Mary and Paul Ritts until recently when they sold their home at 14 Cookman. They have summered regularly at Chautauqua and have presented a show in the Amphitheater.

Mary and Paul have given original puppet shows on TV and have appeared on the "Today Show." They find Chautauqua to be a haven at all seasons. Their son also enjoys returning to Chautauqua.

This typically Victorian house was built c. 1878 by W. H. Bell of Buena Vista, Pennsylvania. The ground on which the house stands was leased from the Institution first by J. M. Edwards of Phillipston, Pennsylvania, on August 22, 1878 for $225. In 1892, Mr. Bell bought the adjoining empty lot (526) from H. A. Massey of Toronto, Canada. He was the grandfather of Raymond Massey, the famous actor.

On the death of Mrs. Ritts' aunt, Mrs. John Thomas, her fifty percent share in the home was bequeathed to Mary (Donnelly) Ritts. Her mother, Mrs. William C. Donnelly, co-owner, decided to give her share to Mary in 1966.

The cottage is corner property and faces the Hall of Philosophy grounds. It is constructed of board and batten and has railings going across the front and side porches. A spacious dwelling, there is gingerbread under the eaves.

Fourteen Cookman was sold in 1975 to Mrs. Barbara B. O'Reilly. The Ritts, although no longer property owners, plan to return to Chautauqua at every opportunity which presents itself.

This row of houses has porches facing the Hall of Philosophy. The one on the lower right, 14 Cookman, is the former summer home of Mary Donnelly Ritts.

21 Palestine
Farwell Cottage

On August 23, 1878, 21 Palestine Avenue was leased to Laura Baldwin Farwell and A. S. and Mary Salisbury. A structure is shown in this location on the map of that date. Mrs. Farwell attended the first Assembly and every one thereafter until her death in 1901. She transferred her rights to the property to Rev. Henry Clay Millman and his wife Florence Farwell Millman in 1897. Laura Farwell was the grandmother of Marjory Farwell. Members of the family have enjoyed the cottage through the years. Marjory was bequeathed the property by her aunt and ran it as a rooming house. She bought 5 Bowman Avenue in 1934.

Farwell Cottage is desirable because of its nearness to the Amphitheater. The front of the cottage faces the back of the Amphitheater. The tenants may sit on the porch and hear programs. Constructed of white clapboard, it is of simple cottage style. The diamond-shaped beveled windows add a distinctive touch. There are five apartments in this cottage.

Marion Rohm purchased the cottage from Marjory Farwell in 1966. Mrs. Rohm is knowledgeable in the antique field and has furnished it in Victorian Cottage style, keeping many traditional Chautauqua pieces.

The Joseph Panebianco family became the owners in 1977.

41

22 Center
"Peony"

One of the houses that catches the eye, on the most picturesque street in Chautauqua, is 22 Center Avenue. "Peony" cottage was erected in 1879 on a tent floor.

Called Victorian Vernacular in architecture, it borrows its Italian Renaissance balustrades from the sixteenth-century.[20] The eaves ornament—a lattice screen—is the handiwork of an anonymous carpenter with great sensitivity and creative ability.

The house is built on a rise with stairs leading up to the porch. The ground floor porch is decorated with classical arcade motif. The main entrance through a center door is flanked by two balanced shuttered windows. The downstairs porch railings are stick crossed. On the left side is a walk leading to a side door into the kitchen.

The house at 22 Center is built of white clapboard. The floor plan consists of a living room across the front with a stairway on the right side leading to the second floor where there are two bedrooms and a bath. Behind the living room is a small dining room with a door to the left leading into the kitchen. There is a small storage room at the back.

The Chautauqua Yearbook of 1895 lists the owners as the L. C. Barkdull Estate of Sidney, Ohio.

Marie and Louise Crouch, whose family built the Lutheran House, sold the cottage to Helen and Fred Theurer in 1969 because they felt the Theurers had a feeling for the cottage. Both Fred and Helen spent many summers at Chautauqua and then became residents at a permanent Chautauqua address.

42

Mrs. Theurer, before her death in 1977, was the former Director of the CLSC and has entertained such prominent speakers as author Alexander Adams and the United Nations Commissioner for UNESCO, Nicholas T. Goncharoff, at the house.

Sixteenth century Italian Renaissance balustrades decorate this Victorian tent-floored house at 22 Center. The tent floor dated from 1876 and the later construction from 1879.

1 Morris Avenue

One Morris Avenue is presently used as the home and office of the resident physician at Chautauqua. It was remodeled from a private home in 1947.

The Victorian house, built in 1879, has wide porches on both the first and second levels. Facing Bestor Plaza, it is located to the right of the Colonnade Building.

The house is built of white clapboard and the original porch railings have been removed and replaced with wrought iron. There is a central entrance leading into the vestibule. On the right is a living room now used for a waiting room with a room behind it. On the left are two rooms used for doctors' offices and behind these is a kitchen with wainscotting walls. There is a back entrance.

A closed stairway leads from the vestibule to the second floor bedrooms. The house was built by Anna Miller. The Rev. Benjamin Franklin Wade, grandfather of Arthur Wade of Cleveland, Ohio, owned the property when the house was moved across the street to make room for the Colonnade Building in 1905. Mr. Arthur Wade now resides at 1 Maple Avenue.

Dr. Garra L. Lester has practiced medicine at Chautauqua since 1937 and has lived in this house since 1947. Winner of the Chautauqua Centennial Medal in 1974, he was associated with Dr. Haskins in the Timberlake house at 12 Vincent when he first came to this area. Previously, medical service had been administered to the community by Dr. Belnap with offices in the Arcade.

This house was chosen by Olaf William Shelgren as typical Chautauqua architecture because of its porches.

23 S. Terrace

The July 18, 1879, the Chautauqua *Assembly Herald* supplement announced the building of a cottage at 23 South Terrace.

Of typical Victorian Gothic architecture, it boasts some characteristic gingerbread trim. Most of this is still intact but some has been replaced.

The house, which was originally a rooming house, has been made into apartments. The structure is two stories high with the second floor having a steep gabled roof based on Gothic form. In the corners of the porch rails is found elaborate carpenter's lace. There are railings on both first and second floor porches. The door on the right leads into the living room.

The main entrance is on the left side of the house and there is a stairway leading to the second floor. This type cottage was featured in A. J. Downing's *Cottage Residences.* It was typical of American cottages of this period. The house is built of clapboard with green shutters. The stairs leading to the basement are on the right hand side.

23 S. Terrace was built in the old section of Chautauqua and is but a few feet from a three-story rooming house on the right hand side. Another two-story house is on the left.

The present owners, John and Marjorie McCandless, purchased the house from Mrs. C. W. Safford. Dr. McCandless is a dentist in Franklin, Pennsylvania.

How They Lived (1880-1881)

In 1880, fifty acres were added to the grounds. The Athenaeum Hotel was projected and begun. Longer seasons and the affluence of permanent Chautauquans led to a rash of home-building. Homes and buildings become larger to accommodate large families and many guests.

A variety of architectural styles dotted the grounds. Guild's steamboat Gothic at 38 S. Lake had wide porches to take advantage of the "clean air" and view of the lake.

The National W.C.T.U. held its sixth anniversary at Chautauqua, and the National Education Association met here.

By 1881, the charming W. H. Bell residence at 14 Cookman extended the boundary of fine homes to Cookman on the south end. The Athenaeum of Gothic with Moorish influence was completed. Further, the new Museum was opened and correspondence courses were chartered.

Chautauqua connected with the Philadelphia R. R. at Buffalo, New York. From Buffalo, Chautauqua-bound passengers arrived at Mayville via train and again, by train, proceeded on to Chautauqua.

16 S. Terrace
Little Austin

The name Little Austin was given to 16 S. Terrace by Mrs. Spencer Smith's sister whose name was Austin. One Chautauquan thinks it should be called "Cookie Cottage." Mrs. Smith's father, Clifton Flenniken, was an engineer and his wife lived in this cottage after his death.

The house is on a half-lot. In the early days the house was owned by Ford and Gale of Stedman, New York. They used it for part of a laundry together with the house next door. The property was originally leased by the Prendergasts.

The laundry of Ford & Gale was located behind the present Longfellow in Chautauqua's early days. 16 S. Terrace formed part of it and is built on a half-lot. The photograph on Roberts and Miller shows the back of the cottage immediately to the left of the tent on the right side of the photo.

It is in the district of the first settlement of the Chautauqua Assembly and is one block from the Amphitheater and two blocks from the lake. There is a vacant lot to the left which has an attractive planting. The house that was built on this corner lot was destroyed by fire.

The house was built circa 1880 and is shown on the 1880 map of the Chautauqua Grounds. The outside of this Gothic cottage with peaked roof is white clapboard. Porches were built on two

levels with railings replaced with wrought iron. There are windows on either side of the center door. They are long and narrow.

On the left side of the house is an entrance into a hallway that leads to the second floor bedrooms. There is a living room across the front with a combination dining room and kitchen behind it. Upstairs are two bedrooms.

The Arthur E. Wades owned the house and sold it to me when they moved to 1 Maple Avenue. I sold it to the present owners, the Wilhoyte family of Columbus, Ohio. The trim was formerly painted dark blue but is presently yellow.

44

38 South Lake
Hukill Cottage

One of the elegant houses shown on S. Lake Drive on the Chautauqua Map of 1880 is the Hukill home. It was the last house located on the south end of Lake Drive. Marked under the name of J. Guild, Mrs. Clara Hukill Leeds, veteran Chautauquan who died in 1975, reported that her family bought the house from the Guilds in 1887.

Mr. George P. Hukill of Oil City, Pennsylvania, was interested in oil. His name is in a floor tile in the Hall of Philosophy. The Hukill family came here in 1881 and stayed at the Ferry Cottage on Simpson. Mr. Hukill was a friend of Bishop James M. Thoburn, 12 Cookman Avenue, who gave the address at the laying of the cornerstone of the Hall of Christ.

The Hukill home is of Steamboat Gothic style with rambling porches on the front and right sides. The mansard roof is brown and gabled like the House of Seven Gables. It covers about two-thirds of the second floor; the other third has a flat porch roof.

There are dormer windows and doors on the third floor. The windows are all long and each has four panes of glass. In 1901, the elaborate gingerbread was removed from around the windows and porches. The entrance is in the center with a bay window on the right side.

The Hukills arrived by horse and carriage to their elegantly decorated, mansard-roofed cottage at 38 South Lake Drive.

The Hukill children played with the Vincent children in the sandbox in front of their house. Sometimes, Bishop Vincent had to warn them about being too noisy on Sunday.

The house is currently painted bright green with white trim. Mrs. Clara Hukill Leeds was an interior decorator and was responsible for the redecoration of the Athenaeum in 1971.

Georgia Hukill of Cleveland and Mrs. Edgar Taylor, niece of the Hukills, reside in the cottage in the summer.

45

12 S. Lake Drive

One of the earliest recollections of Bess Shepherd Morrison was visiting her Grandmother Shepherd at 12 S. Lake Drive across from the William Baker (then the Lebanon). Mrs. Shepherd housed paying guests in this rambling three-story Victorian cottage.

One of the most famous and interesting guests was Georges Miquelle, principal cellist with the orchestra in 1934. Bess says he rented a room on the third floor with two double beds. He slept in one, and—you guessed it—his cello reclined in the other.

The first record of a lease for the cottage was from the Assembly to the Rev. J. W. Whalen, D.D., from Erie in 1873. Built circa 1880, the house was transferred from Mrs. Doris Walker to her daughter Bess Clifton Shepherd in 1920.

This building at 12 S. Lake Drive on the corner of South Lake Drive and Miller Avenue adjoins the old Colonnade guest house in the rear. Georges Miquelle, principal cellist with the orchestra, stayed here in 1934 according to Bess Shephard Morrison.

Twelve South Lake Drive is a rambling, Victorian, three-story white clapboard house. There are porches overlooking the lake on the first and second levels. The shingles resemble diamonds in a deck of playing cards. Ben Karp in his exciting book *Wood Motifs in American Domestic Architecture* declares: "The varied shingle idiom is as much the sign of the Victorian era in America as the other varieties of sawn art ornamentation found on 19th century American houses."[21]

Bess Morrison has contributed greatly to Chautauqua. A prominent officer in the Women's Club, she has been responsible for bringing outstanding speakers for their meetings.

A national figure in the prison reform movement, she served on the Board of the Dallas County Grand Jury Association and the International Juvenile Association. Mrs. Morrison was a captain in the WACs during World War II. In the winter she and Judge Morrison reside in Austin, Texas.

16 Peck Avenue
Log Cabin

One of the intriguing things about the only log cabin on the grounds are the names etched on the soft glass of the window panes. These names of happy Chautauquans of other years include Fred E. Parks, Grace E. Rich, Emma Williams, Fred Eyre (July 26, 1896), S. W. Cook, Grace Rich, Catherine Wilson, Fred M. Rich, Alma Brown, and M. T. Brown (August 28, 1897).

16 Peck Avenue was built in 1880 by Steven Baker. It has tree trunks in Y-formation holding up the first floor front and side porch. This two-story house has steps leading to the porch level. The front entrance is on the left of the porch. A gabled roof extends over the left side with a chimney made of native stone of the left side.

The front door has a latchstring welcoming guests into a large living room. The floors are of original wide-planked hemlock and pine boards secured with handmade nails. The stairway led to "loft" bedrooms. Changes have been made since 1968 when the house was renovated by the new owners, Mr. and Mrs. Charles A. Ferguson of Pittsburgh. The kitchen has been moved to the right side of the front porch.

The "cozy" cabin was the home of the William Kenneth McKnight family of Jamestown until purchased by the Fergusons. Mrs. McKnight was the President of the Bird and Tree Garden Club in 1955 and 1956. The club gave the McKnight Garden in back of Smith Wilkes Hall in her memory. In 1974, her daughter, Mrs. Edward Haupt, renovated the garden in her mother's memory.

46

The only log cabin on the grounds, at 16 Peck Avenue, has the names of early Chautauquans etched on the soft glass of the windowpanes.

11 North Lake (Lot 64)

This charming Gothic Revival house is of special interest because in January 1927 several Indian skeletons were found in the ground while digging for a basement was under way. These skeletons are now in the Buffalo Museum of Science. Cooking utensils and implements have also been found at 9 N. Lake, presently owned by Mrs. Ruth Skinner Hutchins.

Obed Edson's book *History of Chautauqua County,* published in 1894, reports that the tribe of the Eries populated the Chautauqua region until the seventeenth century. It was then that the Senecas of the Iroquois Federation destroyed the Eries in a savage attack.

The Chautauqua Yearbook of 1895 lists Lot No. 5, now known as 11 N. Lake, as owned by Mrs. H. E. Eddy.

This house is built on a rise with the lawn leading to the lake. Steps with a wrought iron rail lead up to a spacious porch of typical Chautauqua Grounds style. It has two doors leading out onto the porch. One is in the center right leading into the living room. The other on the left leads into the dining room. This two-story cottage has a railing on both of the two-story porches. A kitchen and bedroom complete the down-stairs floor. A stairway in the middle of the house leads to the second floor bedrooms. The basement has been made into living quarters.

11 N. Lake is built of board and batten construction and is painted white with dark blue shutters. The windows of this circa 1880 house have small panes.

The house was purchased by the Clark Reeds of Industry, Pennsylvania. Mrs. Reed and her family summer in this cottage.

22 South Lake Drive
The Wensley Guest House

The Wensley Guest House is presently used by Chautauqua to house its speakers and many of its musical artists. Some of the lecturers who have been housed here include Tom Wicker, the Tom Kopels, the Theodore Morrisons, the John Stoessingers, Dr. Henry C. Brooks, and the Karl Menningers. Many of these noted people have brought their families on return visits. Chautauqua, somehow, becomes a magnetic experience.

The Wensley House was built in 1881 by D. M. Waggoner of Ellington, New York. It was first known as "Layfayette" after Layfayette Ecker, Civil War veteran. Originally a rooming house, it was inherited by Lee Parkhurst, nephew of the Waggoners. Miss Mary Cotton owned it from 1922 until 1945. Mrs. H. W. Ingham owned it from 1945 to 1952. Mrs. Nina T. Wensley purchased it in 1952.

In 1966, Mrs. Wensley gave the house to the Chautauqua Institution for a guest house. A great Chautauqua benefactor, she was an active Board Member for several years. Nina was the wife of a Cleveland industrialist.

The Wensley Guest House is located on a choice spot overlooking the lake and has easy access to the Athenaeum Hotel and the Amphitheater. There are porches on the front on all three floors and on the Bowman Avenue side. Railings extend all the way around the porches held by columns. There is easy access to the porches, with doors leading out of the rooms. There are many windows with a view of the lake, and in the peaked gable.

On the Bowman Avenue entrance one enters through a porch into a reception room on the second level. The building is constructed of clapboard and is painted green with white trim. The land slopes down toward the lake with colorful plantings.

The Wensley Guest House at 22 South Lake Drive houses Chautauua performers and has columned porches on two sides.

The interior of this spacious Victorian house was remodeled in 1966 while Mrs. W. G. Edwards was the hostess. The interior was decorated by interested young ladies that were summer residents at Chautauqua. Mrs. Edwards was on the Chautauqua Tent Circuit when she was a young girl. She now resides in Washington, D.C. during the winter with her husband, Col. William Edwards, a retired U.S. Army Officer.

Recently, Dr. Helen Overs, former Dean of Women at Fredonia College, has acted as the hostess at the Wensley House. Guests at the Wensley House have their meals at the Athenaeum.

South Lake Drive
Athenaeum Hotel

One of the few surviving antebellum hotels in America, the Athenaeum Hotel has long been the center of gracious living in Chautauua. In the early days the speakers and dignitaries took their meals at the hotel and were available for conversation.

The Athenaeum was opened in 1881 on the site of the Palace Hotel which was made of tent cloth over a frame divided by muslin partitions. The hotel was built in Gothic style with a Moorish influence. Lewis Miller's plans for the building included one of the first dishwashers known, designed by him. The hotel was built in 60 days.

The tall-columned front porch covers one side of the building and commands a beautiful view of the lake. It is intersected by a side porch on the right side directly in back of the Amphitheater. The porches, decorated with intricate gingerbread, are lined with vacationers rocking in one of the many wicker rockers to be found on the grounds.

One of the towers has been removed from the top, and the inside of the hotel was recently refurbished under the direction of Clara Hukill Leeds. The dining room seats 300 and has old-fashioned roses in the wallpaper motif.

In years past, part of the Chautauqua Symphony Orchestra played on the porch on Old First Night and the front lawn was lit with gay lanterns.

As late as the 1960s, when Robert Merrill's wife called him, they had to send a boy up to his room to ask him to come to the phone. She hung on for what seemed, to her, hours. When Merrill did get down to the phone, she asked him what had kept him so long. He replied, "You'd never believe me."

5-7 Morris
The Beechover

A handsome cupola set atop the house at 7 Morris Avenue, circa 1881, seems to be like the decoration on a wedding cake. It could be seen more advantageously in the fall when the leaves were off the trees. Underneath was found a mansard roof with small windows.

No. 5 has been joined by a passageway and was built before 1881 by J. Thacker according to the Chautauqua *Assembly Herald* of July 30, 1881. It is assumed to be older since it is of board and batten construction.

No. 7 boasted wide porches on both the first and second floors. A strip of carved wood may be found under the bracketed eaves on the sides of the house and under the octagon-shaped roof over the cupola. These cupolas were a natural at Chautauqua because they gave such a spectacular view of the lake.

Another distinctive touch was added with the quoins at the corners of the house. The cupola house was listed as owned by Mrs. C. G. Herrick of Chautauqua and No. 5 owned by Miss Isabel Welch of DeFuniak Springs, Florida, in the *Chautauqua Yearbook of 1895.*

The current owner, Mrs. Anna Denniston, purchased both No. 5 and 7 Morris from William R. Thompson in 1952. The twin houses include 32 rooms and two apartments.

At one time a Mrs. Babcock from New Castle served meals on the first floor of the Beechover. It was formerly called the Niagara. Mrs. Babcock housed her kitchen help in No. 9, which is now a vacant lot.

These houses at the top of the Morris Avenue hill create increasing interest for the architectural delights found all the way down to the lake.

How They Lived (1882-1886)

On August 12, 1882, Recognition Day, the first class (the Pioneers) was graduated. The first organ was installed in the Amphitheater.

In 1883, Prof. William Rainey Harper taught for the first time in the summer school. Concerts were given under the direction of W. F. Sherwin and C. C. Case.

The classes of 1883 and 1885 erected class buildings in 1884. The season was lengthened to 53 days.

The year 1885 found the erection of Normal Hall and the 1882 Class Building. Chautauqua University was chartered by the legislature.

Highlight of 1886 was the completion of the Pier Building and the hanging of the chimes therein. Jewett House was given by Mrs. A. H. Jewett the same year and the Chautauqua School of Physical Education was established.

32 South Lake
Francis Willard House

The Francis Willard House is one of the earliest cottages on the south north end on the lakefront and is a fine example of late Victorian architecture. It was purchased by Miss Anna A. Gordon in 1925 for the W.C.T.U., which according to a letter on file in Smith Library, was organized at Chautauqua in 1874.

32 S. Lake was built in 1883 on a rise overlooking the lake between what is now the Chautauqua Women's Club and the United Methodist Missionary Vacation Home. Steps with a

A delicate piece of Gingerbread at 32 South Lake Drive is the finishing touch to the pointed center gable of the former W.C.T.U. House.

wooden railing lead up to a porch across the front enclosed in a railing of matching sawn art. The main entrance is through double doors located in the center of the porch. Decorated posts in pairs adorn the porches. Most of the windows are long and narrow.

A delicate piece of gingerbread directs one's eyes to the pointed gables and roof.

Each gable has a round window. Brackets support the roof cornice. These gabled units are connected by a bay window unit attached to a rear unit. On the third floor one finds dormer windows decorated with sawn art.

The entrance off the porch leads into the living room. The open stairway to the second floor is located on the right side at the back of the room. The dining room is on the downstairs right and the kitchen in the rear has a gazebo-styled latticed porch.

The Francis Willard Memorial Tiffany Window was moved here from Kellogg Hall in 1924 when the 50th anniversary of the W.C.T.U. was celebrated. For many years this house served as a base for the Woman's Christian Temperance Union. Mrs. James . Haller, former Chautauqua Board member, and her family lived in the house until 1974. She was the daughter of Mrs. Neal Heilman, who was the W.C.T.U. hostess here for many years. Dr. Diane Reed, veteran Chautauquan, is the United Nations representative of the W.C.T.U.

The owner of the lot and probable builder of the house in 1883 was the Chess family from Louisville, Kentucky. They are the makers of Mary Chess perfumes. The present owners are the J. S. Rogers family of New York City.

10 Pratt
Reformed Church House

The building at 10 Pratt Avenue is now owned by the Chautauqua United Church of Christ Society. Located on the corner of Miller and Pratt Avenues, it faces Bestor Plaza and is across from the Smith Memorial Library.

Built in 1883 by J. W. Martin of Franklin, Pennsylvania, it is of typical Chautauqua architecture with many porches and doors. The house has a characteristic Queen Anne, turret-type corner entrance. The stooped first floor doorway is supported by stick style braces. Several steps lead up to the doorway.

Identical porches and railings are found on both streets. These two-story porches have carved lintels, and decorative carpenter's lace on the first floor. The third story peak on Miller Avenue has a decorative piece of sawn art.

The house has an outside stairway leading to the middle of the porch on the Pratt Street side. Lattice work covers the area below the porch. The entrance leads to a reception hall inside with an oak stairway leading to the upper rooms. Of white clapboard construction this building lends variety to the houses in this area.

The house was purchased in 1924 by the United Church of Christ, which also owns the building on the corner of Clark and Bowman where church services are held. 10 Pratt Avenue is used to house missionaries and preachers.

Two stained glass windows add to the charm of this Victorian dwelling at 38 Clark first owned by Frank M. Fox. Mr. Fox was a bodyguard of President Lincoln's body when it was taken to Fort Stevens.

38 Clark Avenue
The Norwood

The Norwood at 38 Clark, of Gothic Revival architecture with some gingerbread, is reported to have been built by a Mr. Wescott in 1884. The architect is unknown.

A charming Victorian dwelling, it lays claim to two stained glass windows. It is of typical Chautauqua architecture with porches and doors on two levels. This gives easy access to the out-of-doors.

Mrs. Kay C. Nuttall, granddaughter of Frank M. Fox, the original owner, has related some exciting facts about her grandfather. Mr. Fox served four years in the Union Army during the Civil War. At the age of 16 he enlisted in "Penn Bucktails" and was in the bodyguard when President Lincoln's body was taken to Fort Stevens. Mr. Fox built Alumni Hall, Normal Hall, and the Chaney House at 18 Cookman. His grandson Kenneth Baker owned the Baker Hotel near Palestine Park for many years.

Mr. and Mrs. Leonard S. Smith of Shaker Heights, Ohio, are the present owners.

31 Janes
Foulke Cottage

The Rev. Charles W. Foulke purchased the land and his wife made a tent which was erected on the property each year until 1884. The Rev. Foulke, an experienced carpenter and builder according to a journal kept by his wife, built a house on the lot in 1884.

Isabel Welch purchased the property from the Foulkes in 1889 when they built a home at 32 Janes. Descendants of the Foulkes still own this house. Clergyman Foulke not only participated in religious activities at Chautauqua but also at Findley Lake Lakeside Assembly.

The cottage is located on a triangle-shaped park, one block from the Amphitheater and Smith Wilkes Hall, across from the Gingerbread Cottage. The cottage is still on the original tent site and has not been altered. The construction is of light wood framing with clapboard siding. At the present time it is painted two shades of green.

There is a porch across the front and the roof goes up to a peak in typical cottage style. There are porch railings on both floors indicating a later period.

Entrance to the living room is through a hall with the kitchen and a bedroom and bath at the back. A stairway from the hall leads to the second floor bedroom.

For many years the house was owned by Mrs. Zoe Lafferty and was called "Zoe's Ark." In 1972, it was purchased by the James Mead family of Westfield, New York. Mr. Mead is from a prominent political family and serves as a county supervisor. He is the Editor of the *Westfield Republican,* which also prints the *Chautauquan Daily.*

THE LUCAS COTTAGE

20 Forest Avenue
Pansy Home

The house at 20 Forest Avenue is called the Pansy Home in honor of "Pansy" McDonald Alden.

Mrs. G. R. Alden gained national fame in the Victorian era with her over 100 books, several of which were about Chautauqua. *Four Girls at Chautauqua* was so popular that it brought large numbers of people to Fair Point. Mrs. Alden, the wife of a Presbyterian minister, was present at the Assembly of 1874 and took an active interest in Chautauqua. She continued to spend her summers there until 1895.

The Pansy Home is of Victorian style and was built in 1884 by Anna H. Stewart of Battle Creek, Michigan. It was purchased in 1892 by the Rev. G. R. Alden, of Washington, D.C., whose name was on the deed as late as 1913. David M. Lucas, the present owner, purchased it in 1965. Mrs. Lucas collects dishes decorated with pansies.

The house is located on the corner of Forest and Pratt to the left of the Ravine and across the street from Norton Hall and the Hurlbut Church. It is also next to 19 McClintock Avenue. "Pansy" built the house at 6 Ames Avenue and owned another house at 37 Janes Avenue.

Of shingle construction, this capacious house has a steep roof with gables and mullioned windows and recalls the informal late Medieval country house. It has been slightly altered by the removal of the wooden railing around both porches and the addition of metal railings. The porch roof was removed on the second floor to make a sun deck.

One question: What would "Pansy" write today about the modern girls at Chautauqua?

"Pansy" McDonald Alden, prolific Chautauqua author, owned this rambling Victorian house at 20 Forest from 1892 until 1913.

How They Lived (1887-1891)

The College Building and the Methodist Episcopal House were erected in 1887. A School of Music and a School of Physical Culture were opened.

In 1888, Mr. George E. Vincent became Vice President of Instruction. The Chautauqua Women's Club was organized with Mrs. Emily Huntington Miller as President.

James Kellogg built Kellogg Hall in 1889 as a tribute to his mother. The old Administration Building was erected. President Rutherford B. Hayes visited Chautauqua.

In 1890 the C.L.S.C. Alumni Hall was completed, and the Arcade, the Chapel, and the United Presbyterian House were erected.

39 Palestine

Thirty nine Palestine Avenue just made it inside the original western boundary of the Assembly Grounds. Horses of Chautauquans were quartered in this area in the earliest days. This house is close to the center of activities which developed up on the hill approximately two or three years after the Assembly began.

A well, which is now plugged on the south end of the property, was a source of drinking water. A Mrs. Eddy or Mrs. Grimm had the well water piped into the back porch. About 1969, the old kitchen pump was removed.

The house has an upstairs porch with gingerbread decoration in true Victorian style, with porches extending across the front on both levels. The two different types of gingerbread on the porches indicate that the porches were not constructed at the same time.

The original structure is thought to be T-shaped with a partial cellar. On the right hand side there is a gabled roof with a window in the center. On the left to the rear is another gable with two windows. There are eight bedrooms above and two rooms below. The back section, which houses a kitchen, laundry, bedroom and back porch, was added later. Whether the gingerbread and upstairs porch are original is not definite. The south upstairs porch was subsequently enclosed. The fireplace was added later. The original portion was built circa 1887.

Porch railings varied in design break the regularity of this homey gabled cottage located at 39 Palestine on the site of the early hitching grounds.

The house was purchased in 1955 by the F. B. Irwins of Franklin, Pennsylvania. Mr. Irwin is a prominent lawyer and Mrs. Irwin is the Editor of the *Chautauquan Daily.* The house is very much alive with the gaiety of the members of the Irwin family and their many friends.

Six Miller Park was remodeled in 1947 to combine a porch with Gothic peaks and gables with a horizontal type house.

6 Miller Park

According to the map of 1873 there was a dwelling on the space now known as 6 Miller Park. This structure was used by the members of the Chautauqua Assembly. The date of construction of the present house was 1887 (as reported in the *Assembly Herald*). It was listed in the Chautauqua Yearbook of 1895 under the name of Mrs. J. H. McCray.

This Eclectic type cottage was completely remodeled in 1947. It has white shingle wood frame construction with narrow strips trimmed in gray. A porch running across the front is of Gothic quality with peaks and gables. Even the dormer window is made up of small panes. The columned porch posts add a classical touch.

The John Brandon Campbell family of Tucson, Arizona are the present owners, using it for a summer home. The building faces Miller Park—the area known to be the original site of Chautauqua.

The house is adjacent to 4 Miller Park, with Preston Avenue running in between and 8 Miller Park on the other side.

53

8 Miller Park (Lot 26)

The owner at 8 Miller Park was listed in 1871 under the name of H. R. McClintock of Meadville, Pennsylvania, and Hannah Barber of Stockton in 1873. The date of the original cottage was 1887. The present cottage was built by Claude Arnold.

It was then owned by the Rev. R. H. Holmes, according to a letter dated 1877.

The picture of Miller Park in 1873 shows some buildings already in existence. 8 Miller Park may have been a rebuilt structure from this early date. The houses on both sides are very close, and there is a towering maple in front of the porch. In 1889, Miss Alice S. and Miss Margaret B. Veach purchased the property.

Of Gothic Revival style, it has porches on the first and second floors. Railings are broken by Doric columns and there are recessed columns against the front. This vertical house is of board and batten construction. The gabled roof has a delicate piece of gingerbread in its peak. There are two steps leading up to the porch with a center window on both floors and doors on each side of the windows. Unbelievable as it may seem, this house has six bedrooms. The cottage is painted blue with white trim.

The cottage is owned by Robert O. Wilder of New York City. The Wilders are close friends of artist Maritza Morgan and were responsible for her first religious painting commission.

20 Simpson
The Aldine

Mrs. Susie Birch Jennings, friend and companion of Clara Barton of Red Cross fame and a great Chautauqua worker, was at the Aldine in 1897 to look after the personal comforts of the guests. Located across from the Athenaeum Hotel on Simpson and Bowman, 20 Simpson was built by S. B. Jennings of Washington, D.C. in 1887. Here the warm hospitality of Chautauqua was experienced on several occasions by visitors.

The Aldine boasts five stories if the tower of this rooming house is counted. Chautauqua architecture early followed the idea of going up several stories when ground was at a premium. The many porches and windows command a view of the lake.

The porch railings have spindles and posts supporting the sawn art decoration. Brackets hold up the gabled roof of this gray clapboard dwelling.

In 1912, Louise Emmons of Buffalo and her sister, Bernice Fairbanks, bought the property from a bank in Mayville. It was run by Mrs. Fairbanks' niece, Irene King, from 1966 to 1971. The Aldine was purchased in 1971 by the Robert Grays who run it as a rooming house.

41 Pratt Avenue

Mrs. Hester Ringling Sanford, member of the famous Ringling circus family, bought a summer cottage at 41 Pratt Avenue in 1939. Since 1972, it has been owned by Charles and Alice Lancaster.

The original house was built in 1907 for Dean Percy H. Boynton, of the University of Chicago, by Jewett and Plaisted. Dean Boynton later was appointed and served as Principal of the Summer Schools until 1917. Dr. Hurlbut gives him credit for much of the success of the schools. In 1916, Dr. Boynton gave a series on "The Growth of Consciousness in American Literature." We can only conjecture that Dr. Boynton chose Lots 1138 and 1130 because this corner is adjacent to College Park and has a spectacular view of the lake. Many vines covered the porches, giving privacy and protection from the summer sun.

This brown-shingled cottage has a gambrel roof (pentagonal). The origin of the common use of this roof was believed to have been to obtain greater headroom in the upper floor. Popular in the Northeast, this Dutch type roof was widely used in New York State. It was a highly advantageous style in Chautauqua. The gables at the end walls provided space for windows. The Lancasters have cited "squirrels" as the only threat to the building.

A guest house was built in 1920. Major alterations of the house were made in 1971. The Children's Room of Smith Library has a circus theme, and it is only fitting to have descendants of this distinguished family of the entertainment world as cottage holders.

The Charles Lancasters, members of the famous Ringling Circus family, summer in this vine covered cottage at 41 Pratt. It was built in 1907 for Percy Boynton of the University of Chicago.

One of the most elegant Victorian cottages on the grounds is located at 1 Irving. The pointed roof of the porch forms a cupola and gives a most advantageous view of the lake.

1 Irving Place

The entrance to the railroad station that connected with Mayville trains was located at the foot of Root Avenue in the area of 1 Irving Place.

High on a bank with a superb view of the lake, this Victorian house has a porch with a roof going up to a peak on four sides. There is a turret on the right side and a peaked gable on the left side of the roof covering the second story. A lovely garden in the back is on street level.

Dr. and Mrs. Louis Meisse are the present residents. Dr. Meisse is an atomic scientist in Jamestown, New York. Mary Meisse is a past president of the Friends of Smith Library.

They purchased the house in 1966 from Mrs. Eugene McCartry who had purchased the property from Mrs. Florence Roblee in 1943. Mrs. Roblee was related to the producers of Roblee shoes. Chautauqua Trustee Mrs. Richard Duhme, Jr., is a daughter of the Roblees. She and her family summered at 1 Irving Place until they purchased a cottage at 1522 Oak Avenue. The Duhme's house was moved across the road to a lakefront lot in 1976.

In 1919, Mr. James H. Prendergast of Westfield had owned the house. The first transaction had been in 1888 from the Assembly to William Mulkee as Trustee for M. Manderville and W. L. Darling. The house was built circa 1888.

55

Mrs. S. E. Grassie, one of the first graduates of the CLSC, was listed as the owner of 9 Root Avenue in *The Chautauqua Yearbook of 1895.* Of Victorian Vernacular architecture, it has a decorative bay window in the center of the first floor porch.

9 Root
The Rochester

The house at 9 Root Avenue was originally owned by Mrs. S. E. Grassie. One of the first graduates of the Chautauqua Literary and Scientific Circle, she was very active in its work. Mrs. Grassie lived to be a hundred years old. One of her close friends was Mrs. Thomas A. Edison.

The house was built in 1887 and Alfred Cowles of Larder, Pennsylvania was the builder. *The Chautauqua Yearbook of 1895* lists Mrs. Grassie of Cambridgeboro, Pennsylvania as the owner.

This Victorian Vernacular cottage boasts of side porches with railings, a bay window on the front of the house, posts holding up the second floor porch, and a balcony area on the right third floor. Gingerbread over the doors and sawn art shingles give it a Victorian look.

The house, painted white, is built close to No. 7 owned by Lewis Petitt and No. 11 purchased in 1975 by the Bernard Taylors from the J. H. Seebachs.

This area faces a ravine and is near to Norton Hall. It is the summer residence of the Roger Triskets, its present owners.

This picture of 40 S. Lake was taken before renovation about 1910. Chautauqua presidents W. G. Hickman and Judge W. Walter Braham have lived here.

40 S. Lake Drive

Although altered from its original style, this house is historic in that two Chautauqua presidents have lived here. It also has the distinctive Chautauqua characteristic of easy access to the out-of-doors. Porches on both levels facing the lake must have made entertaining a pleasure to both President W. G. Hickman and Judge W. Walter Braham.

Located on the corner of S. Lake Drive and Cookman Avenue, this white vine-covered cottage was built in 1888. W. Wheeler, a U.S. Congressman from Pennsylvania, was the original owner. Isabel Pederson, Judge Braham's daughter, writes: "It was a better example of Carpenter's Gothic style before the remodeling." Mrs. Pederson reports extensive changes between 1910 and 1920. The original one-floor porch was replaced by present two floor porches, the Alpine-type balconies and third-floor doors, and much Gingerbread, were removed.

Some board and batten was replaced by clapboard. Fortunately, some of the original gingerbread at the back of the house and the original scroll motif over the windows have been retained.

The house has been adapted to the lakeside location and climate. Railings with decorative spindles extend around the front and left sides. Simple columns support the stately porch.

According to Miss Georgia Hukill, next door neighbor, there was a huge sand pile covered by an awning in front of 38 and 40 S. Lake Drive in the 1890s.

The house at 38 Miller Park was built in 1889 and is now owned by the Robert Wadells. Mrs. Wadell is a member of the Heinz family who has summered at Chautauqua for many years.

38 Miller Park (Lot 44)

The residence at 38 Miller Park is now lively with the Robert N. Wadell, Jrs., and their five children in residence. Mrs. Wadell, née Heinz, and other members of her well-known family have cottages at Chautauqua. They all hail from Pittsburgh. The Wadells studied the history of Chautauqua for their 1976 Bicentennial project.

This Victorian type house was built in 1889 by C. W. and Sara A. Sanford of Westfield, New York, who purchased the lease in 1888. Mrs. Lizzie Kidd of New York held the lease from 1892 to 1896 when the property passed to Mrs. Irene C. Ritts of Butler, Pennsylvania, who extensively remodeled it.

A porch extends across the front and on the right side. The gables go up to a peak on the front and side with a slanted roof over the porch. There are pieces of sawn art in the peaks and a turret on the front of the roof. The house is gray with white trim and has awnings inside the columned porches and over the front porch door. The front faces Vincent Avenue and extends around on to Simpson Avenue.

The house is located on Simpson Avenue and Miller Park. There are no houses on the adjacent lot on the Miller Park side and 4 Simpson is on the Simpson side. The Wadells purchased the house from Mrs. Ritts in 1972.

9 Palestine
United Presbyterian
Headquarters

Dr. Jesse L. Hurlbut, writing in his book, *The Story of Chautauqua* (1890), states: "This was the year when the Presbyterian house was opened. …" With its first brick building begun in 1889, Chautauqua was heading in the direction of more stable and impressive buildings, yet it was still in its formative years.

Architect Olaf William Shelgren chose this as one of the best examples of Chautauqua porches for our historical survey. He selected it because the back of the building which overlooks Smith-Wilkes Hall has wide open porches as well as both levels on the front. The front faces the Amphitheater. When outstanding artists play to Standing Room Only, fortunate Chautauquans may look and listen from the Palestine Avenue porches.

Presbyterian Headquarters is of brick with white wooden trim similar to Georgian buildings. The back porch has wide pillars with Doric columns giving it the stately quality of a temple commonly found in Greek Revival buildings.

One notes that it borrows from many styles and may be labeled "Vernacular." The roof rises to a peak with white clapboard in the peak and a narrow window with small panes in the entablature on the Janes Avenue side.

On the ground level in the rear is an entrance into a dining room. At the left of this entrance is a planting in memory of Mrs. Roy Mapes—a dedicated church-woman and Chautauquan.

Headquarters were remodeled in the 1960s mainly through the efforts of the Clyde L. Carnahans. Presbyterians gather on Sunday at nine-thirty in the morning to worship in the first floor Chapel which seats 200. The second floor bedrooms accommodate missionaries from both the home and foreign fields.

This Victorian dwelling at 41 Lake Drive was the former home of Mrs. Elizabeth McCreery who gave the "Spirit of Chautauqua" bus. It has had the porches enclosed to enlarge the living room.

41 N. Lake Drive

Located on the lake front near Miller Park is 41 N. Lake Drive. It was built by Mrs. Jessie C. Loomis of Cleveland, Ohio in 1890. On the left is found the Clement Studebaker house and on the right is the Farrar house.

The original house is typically Victorian with a wide porch overlooking the lake. Decorative columns support the porch roof on the front and left sides. The front side has open porches with arches over the columns on the second floor. The roof on two sides go up to a peak. Inside the peaks there are goups of windows on the third floor. The Myron Johnson, Jrs., house adjoins the property on the McClintock Avenue side.

The house is built of white clapboard with sawn art shingles. It is built on a bank with a planting of flowers and shrubs.

Remodeled by the Spencer Smiths in 1961, it is a fine example of adaptive use. The front porch was enclosed with glass to make a large living room. Richard Wilcox was the builder. The architect was the owner, a graduate of Yale School of Architecture. A retired Navy Admiral, he was in charge of the Seabees in the Pacific during World War II.

On August 15, 1955, Mrs. Elizabeth McCreery purchased the property. Mrs. McCreery was a trustee and benefactor of Chautauqua. She gave the bus, "The Spirit of Chautauqua," on which one may ride around the grounds for ten cents.

The Spencer Smiths purchased the home in 1961. Mrs. Smith, the former Bette Flenniken of Hamburg, New York, attended school in Hamburg where her father, an engineer, built many houses.

The Smiths owned "The Little White House" at 17 Roberts until they purchased 41 N. Lake Drive. They, with their five children, live in Hawaii but are frequently in residence at Chautauqua.

43 N. Lake Drive

The first home to be electrified on the Chautauqua grounds was the one at 43 N. Lake Drive, according to Mr. Charles Case, a protégé of Thomas Edison. He was the grandson of Charles S. Farrar, of Akron, the original builder of the house. Case and the Farrars were friends of the Edisons. Mr. Case worked with Mr. Edison at his factory in West Orange, New Jersey.

They had to wait three years after the electricity was wired into the house to have the lights turned on because there was no generator at Chautauua. Mrs. Leslie Bowman, daughter of Mr. Case, lived at 63 Palestine until 1974. She says that a generator was installed at the Amphitheater and service was available on the grounds.

The house has a beautiful view of the lake and is located on a corner lot with Hurst Avenue on the right side and the Spencer Smith house on the left. It is a typical Victorian style house with first floor porch.

A railing with wide posts supports the porch roof, which has a cupola in the center. The house is built of green clapboard.

The initial construction dates from July 21, 1890. It was purchased on November 27, 1937, by Charles H. Williams and his wife of Bradford, Pennsylvania. John H. Rogers and his sister, Helene, who lived in the house at the time of the Historic Site Survey, are relatives of Frances Willard.

14 Vincent Avenue
St. Elmo Hotel

The St. Elmo Hotel is one of the centers of year-round activity. In the summer season it is alive with the people who come for the season's program. Off-season, it caters to those who like to be close to nature, read, ski, play bridge, do puzzles, and just enjoy Chautauqua.

The exterior of the main building of the St. Elmo is of neo-Georgian architecture with three turn-of-the-century Victorian homes attached. The original house, which has an entrance on Vincent and Pratt Avenues, was built in the 1890s and used as a residence until 1896. The addition to this building was made in 1918. The two private homes were attached in 1910.

The main building has a portico with classical columns. Long windows, with small panes, frame the entrance. Above the door is a transom with small window panes. Dormer windows are found in the slanted roof. There is an enclosed porch with an overhanging cornice on Pratt Avenue extending to the side entrance of the house, which was one of those attached in 1910.

The main edifice has three floors and 90 rooms. The trim of the buildings is white and the wood is painted red. The dining room of the St. Elmo has an entrance on Ames and Pratt Avenues. A balcony for private parties is available in the back of the dining room and there are windows along Ames Avenue.

Accommodations are also available in the charming small former Presbyterian Chapel and in the house next to it for guests of the St. Elmo. The Chapel has an entrance with arches supporting the porch roof. The Victorian house, immediately adjacent, was added in 1910.

This "Steamboat Gothic" house at 45 North Lake has a porch the full length of the front. It was built by Dr. Theodore Flood, Editor of the *Chautauquan*.

There are some notable furnishings of the period in the St. Elmo complex. Of special interest is the fireplace in the Main Lounge which personifies the quotation: Burning logs give back the glow Of summer suns long ago.

The hotel has an abundance of gaily upholstered wicker furniture. It is a delight to pull one of the chairs up by the fire on a snowy night.

The dormitory, used to house staff, of the St. Elmo is located at 11 Roberts Avenue. The St. Elmo has long been known for taking a personal interest in their guests. The Brown family and the Bates family created this atmosphere. Many retired people make their year-round home here. At publication date, the St. Elmo is owned by S. J. and N. S. Nassif.

45 North Lake Drive

This "Steamboat Gothic" house lends variety to Chautauqua architecture. Located on the lakefront, it has easy access to the out-of-doors. The porch, which runs full length of the front and around to the side, was partly enclosed in 1892. There is, also, a "retreat porch" where it is said "men would retreat and then disappear uptown when women talked too long on the front side."

Forty five N. Lake Drive was built by Dr. Theodore Flood, Editor of the *Chautauquan Weekly,* in 1890. Dr. Flood was a printer from Meadville. Wood siding was put on the house between 1969 and 1971. Two furnaces were also installed. In 1954, the kitchen was completely remodeled.

There are cupolas or turrets above the porch at each end of the house. The outside is painted white. The interior walls are of wood, and the only plaster in the house is on the chimneys. An open stairway leads out of the spacious living room to the second floor. The kitchen is at the rear of the house with a downstairs bedroom on the right side of the house. The rest of the sleeping rooms are on the second floor.

The house was purchased in 1900 by Mrs. Caroline King, wife of Dr. Rufus King and grandmother of Mrs. Frank Karslake and Julius King. Her daughter, Mrs. Virginia Gilkey, and grandson Ezra Gilkey owned it until 1958 when it passed out of the King family and was purchased by Mr. George Cornell. Dr. and Mrs. King traveled extensively, and the house is filled with ceramic and brass pieces brought from all over the world. There is a washstand known as President McKinley's washstand. He used it when he was a guest in the house.

Mr. Cornell has been an active member of the Chautauqua Board of Trustees. Mrs. Helen Cornell is past president of the Friends of Smith Library.

59

34 Janes Avenue
Gingerbread Cottage

Gingerbread Cottage, my summer home, is the most photographed and painted house on the grounds. Of American Gothic architecture, it boasts intricate gingerbread. Built in 1891, both builder and designer are unknown.

The house at 34 Janes is built on a tent platform. It typifies the simple way early Chautauquans lived. There is an upstairs and downstairs porch with two doors leading out to each. This gives the occupants the easy access to the out-of-doors typical of early Chautauqua houses.

Built as a guest house, it was occupied by the Carrier family for five generations. A. J. Carrier came with his wife from Lockport, New York. The house passed from Mr. Carrier to his daughter and then to her daughter, Amy Crane Buchanan. Finally, Amy Buchanan's son sold it to the writer, Chautauqua's Librarian for 14 years.

The location of Gingerbread Cottage on a corner across from Lincoln Park draws attention to it. Many people stop by to sit in the red rocker and have their pictures taken.

60

Early photograph of owner A. J. Carrier and guest shows vine covered porch at 34 Janes extending almost over to the side porch of 32 Janes. This was one of the smallest early lots.

The old pine walls have been preserved in the living room. A small sitting room on the left side of the house in back of the living room now has a green and white tent ceiling. The bedroom has been made into a kitchen with a pass-through for dishes into the sitting room. A sink has been installed. The drain, still in the backyard, was formerly the only piped in sink. A shed on the back was originally a summer kitchen, but the floor was too uneven to keep the pans on the stove.

I have removed an upstairs wall to enlarge the bedroom. The original rooms housed only a single bed and dresser with a typical Chautauqua closet. This was a board fastened to the wall with a curtain around it. Doors were held back by rocks tied with red or blue bandanas. I have also installed a furnace to make it livable in winter.

This small guest house, now painted white with green shutters, was formerly gray with red trim. It is representative of the accommodations offered during the Gay Nineties period when Chautauqua played a stellar role in the cultural, spiritual, and recreational part of the American scene. Together with the many other houses of this period, it forms an important link to this unit.

Many accomplished people have tarried here. They include Thyra Ferre Bjorn, Margaret Widdemer, Theodore Morrison, Paula Bishop, Eda LeShan, Karl and Jean Menniger, Russell Welch, Clifford Harvuot, Bess and Judge "Bill" Morrison, Consul General and Mrs. Ivar Gudmundsson of Iceland, and all the Fanchers.

This detail of the front of Gingerbread Cottage at 34 Janes, picturing the gable and bargeboards, was taken by Ken Marsh, a childhood Jamestown friend.

This Victorian cottage at 23 Morris has a lovely ravine to the right. On the left are the porches of 19 Morris as they were in nineteenth-century Chautauqua.

23 Morris (Lot 215)
Kimball Cottage

Elizabeth Bishop of Chicago, who brought the Delsartian Calisthenic System to the Assembly, built the house at 23 Morris Avenue circa 1891. She was an elocutionist and gave demonstrations in the Amphitheater.

On the original site with a ravine flowing in back of the house, it was built on the corner of Morris Avenue and North Lake Drive. The owners call it "early Hallowe'en" in architecture, but it has Victorian style characteristics.

This private dwelling has a sun porch at the right end with seven sleeping rooms on the second floor. The porch was enclosed by the Kimballs. The bedrooms are furnished with brass and iron beds and have typical grass matting on the floors. The front stoop covers a pair of double doors with transom of small panes of glass above the doors. These small panes of glass are also used in the upper part of the other windows.

Entering the sun porch we find the furniture is all of old wicker. This room leads into the small entrance hall which goes into the dining room. A whole china cupboard of pre-World War I blue willow ware from Japan is found in this room. To the left is the kitchen and a stairway leading to the second floor. The house has gray clapboard siding.

The Guernsey family of Kansas City bought the house from Mrs. Bishop in 1917. The Kimballs purchased it in 1930. Mrs. George Thatcher Guernsey returned to 23 Morris on July 26, 1972, when she was President General of the National Society of the DAR. The Hon. and Mrs. Charles N. Kimball brought their family here summers. Mr. Kimball was Supreme Court Justice of West Virginia.

Mrs. Floyd Haker and her brother are the present owners. Mrs. Haker is a former President of the Bird, Tree and Garden Club. She states that their property has the second largest beech tree on the Chautauqua Grounds. Mrs. Haker and her husband, an inventor, reside in Dallas, Texas, in the winter.

61

How They Lived (1892-1901)

The year 1892 was the most successful one yet known at Chautauqua. The Chautauqua System of Education was substituted for Chautauqua University.

The year 1893 saw the erection of many new buildings: the new Amphitheater, the electric light and power plant, the sewage disposal plant, and the Men's Club House.

The Episcopal Chapel of the Good Shepherd was built in 1894. It was the first year of the School of Expression under Prof. S. W. Clark and Mrs. Emily M. Bishop.

In 1895, Higgins Hall was erected by the Hon. Frank W. Higgins and his sister, Mrs. F. S. Smith, in memory of their father, Orin Trail Higgins. The Baptist House was also built.

The School of Fine Arts and the New York State Summer Institute for Teachers were new features in 1896.

The year 1897 saw the opening of the School of Domestic Sciences of Mrs. Emma P. Ewing, and also saw the erection of the Hall of Pedagogy. Prof. George E. Vincent became Principal of Instruction.

The Boys' Club building, the Chautauqua Press, and the establishment of the General Endowment Fund emerged in 1899.

The first year of our century, 1900, was the year of the Auli Christi beginning and the Power House was built.

The Chautauqua School of Library Training was established under Melvil Dewey, Father of the Dewey System.

And so concluded the Victorian Period.

This Carpenter Gothic house at 11 Morris is painted in two shades of green in true Victorian style. Famed artist Will Smedley had his studio here.

11 Morris Avenue

Eleven Morris Avenue was the home of Chautauqua's distinguished artist-naturalist-writer, Will Lary More Smedley. Mr. Smedley, listed in *Who's Who,* was a member of the National Academy. His paintings are housed at 11 Morris Avenue where his widow and daughter, Thaline Brewer, reside year round.

Morris Avenue is one of the oldest streets in Chautauqua. High on a knoll, the Carpenter's lace in the corners of the post railings of the Smedley house is much admired by passers-by. There are large beech trees surrounding this Gothic Revival dwelling, and a ravine is found behind it.

The house was built circa 1889 and is of original board and batten white pine construction. The light green paint contrasts with its darker green trim. The porch on the north side has been enclosed during the last 40 years to match the cottage. The railings on both the first and second floors are decorated with spindles.

The entrance to the front door leads into the living room where Will Smedley, an architect turned painter, painted as early as 1894. His easel, made by him of mahogany, usually stands with the light shining on it. Mark Twain was one of his correspondents and admirers.

Behind the front room is a dining room and kitchen. The bedrooms are upstairs.

The house is a museum of love to one of Chautauqua's first artists. His seascapes, portraits, and landscapes in oil may be seen in Smith Library and in many Chautauqua homes.

Chapel of the Good Shepherd at Wythe and Park is a Gothic Episcopal Chapel with an unusual hood over the entrance, patterns of scalloped shingles, narrow arched windows, and black hinged vestible doors. It invites you to enter and be thankful.

This rambling Victorian cottage at 4 Vincent has an abundance of porches with views of the lake. Can't you just see it decorated with flower pots when it was a flower shop?

Wythe and Park
Chapel of the Good Shepherd

The Chapel of the Good Shepherd is located on the corner of Clark and Park Avenues next to the Grove on the south end of the grounds near the Hall of Philosophy. Completed in 1894, it was the fifth building erected for denominational worship.

Of Old English style of Gothic architecture, it boasts a stained single roof and projecting bell hood. Under the hood is an arched window with cut shingles, the rows of shingles forming a pattern that emphasizes the window.

The veranda in the front of this jewel of a building goes up to a peak topped by a cross. The entrance has double doors with wrought iron hinges and two windows above. Steps with railings lead to the entrance.

The interior is lighted by cathedral glass windows. The assembly of the Chapel measures 25 by 46 feet. The Chapel is painted white and is set off by the greenery of this end of the grounds.

Administered by St. Paul's Episcopal Church in Mayville, it seats 150 people. This miniature church is used for services during the season and for weddings off-season.

4 Vincent
Sunny Verandas

"Sunny Verandas" boasts of having been a flower shop and an antique shop as well as rooming house. Hearsay has it that Mrs. Wilcox of Sherman, New York, used to pile row upon row of potted plants on the hillside corner in the 1930s.

Kenneth and Mary Slorpe obtained a lease or deed to the property in 1953, and Mrs. Slorpe operated an antique shop here. Located on the corner of Terrace and Vincent, immediately behind the Miller Cottage, it was convenient to the Auditorium, the Pavillion, and the first Boarding House where many people ate. The present Post Office now stands on this site.

The Rev. W. J. Barton's name is found in an *Assembly Herald* and also in an Assembly publication's listing of properties in connection with No. 4 Vincent in 1895 and 1903.

In 1957 the house was purchased by Robert and Robin Seasted. Mr. and Mrs. Harold E. Boehm purchased it from them in 1962.

This rambling Victorian Vernacular house is a typical Chautauqua style with easy access to the out-of-doors. It was originally of board and batten construction. This has now been covered with brown shingles.

Six windows were covered up and there were doors leading out onto the verandas from the choicest rooms. These rooms have been made into a rental apartment on the third floor and winterized family quarters have been made on the first and second floors. There are sawn art railings on the first and third floors. A corner turret adds variety.

The living room has been enlarged by installing large thermoglass windows to include the front and side verandas. The entrance has been changed to the upper front side and a new walk and patio installed.

Mr. Boehm is presently Director of Business and Finance of the Federation for Community Planning for Cleveland. He and his wife hope to make "Sunny Verandas" their year-round retirement home.

63

The Cary has added buildings across the street connected by a walkway to the original building. An elevator in the form of a tower, installed later, gives a new touch to this gambrel-roofed building.

46 S. Lake (Merrill and S. Lake) Booth Cottage

Forty six S. Lake Drive is the home of Miss Helen Booth, sister of Edwin Prince Booth, nationally known author and theologian. The cottage overlooking the lake on South Lake and Merrill was built prior to 1895. Lot 616 was listed under the name of Miss A. R. Murphy of Philadelphia in *The Chautauqua Yearbook of 1895.*

The Booths came to Chautauqua as children to visit their mother's cousins, Mrs. Margaret McKelvy and Mrs. Youngson, at the corner of McClintock and Andrews. Mrs. Youngson helped with the Normal School at Chautauqua from 1900 until 1925. From 1925 until 1939 they rented during the summer.

In 1939 Helen's brother Bill bought 46 S. Lake Drive, selling it to her in 1949. Her brother Ted (Edwin) and children visited Helen at her home. Francis Booth, Helen's nephew, an architect in New York and James H. Cook, Pittsburgh, spoke on the "Architecture of Chautauqua" in the Amphitheater in 1968.

The Booth Cottage at 46 S. Lake is one of many large, elegant cottages on South Lake Drive. Many of these Gay Nineties houses had a sense of permanence not seen in the earlier era. Author Edwin Prince Booth stayed here.

A large white cottage with wide porches across the front of the house at 46 S. Lake combines many shapes of Victorian architecture. On the right is a rounded turret covered with a shingled peak, and on the left is a two story turret.

The house is entered through the Merrill Street end of the porch. The second floor is supported by square columns, and the porch has been enclosed to make a bedroom.

Helen Booth had a cathedral window removed from the south side of the house so that the boys could get out in case of fire. One of the boys said: "Don't chop down the tree—I use it for my fire escape."

There is a fireplace in the living room, and the walls are still of board and batten construction. Old marble dressers and washbasins may be found in the interior. Miss Booth is an active member of the Bird, Tree and Garden Club.

9-11-13 Bowman The Cary

The Cary Hotel is an example of Second Empire style which was extremely popular for buildings in the late nineteenth century. There are several examples of this style on the grounds. Built in 1896, this hotel consists of many units joined together. The Bowman Avenue building has a mansard roof.

There is a square elevator shaft on the Wythe Avenue side of the main building. Adjoining this is a porch which has wrought iron railing and posts. The door enters into a reception hall and the main dining hall is beyond the desk. It juts out flush with the street and has a street entrance on Bowman. This three-story building is constructed of clapboard. It is painted white on the first two stories and green on the third.

The windows have narrow panes. There is a hipped roof on the Bowman and Palestine side of the building. The overpass leads to a building on the right at 33 and 35 Miller Avenue.

In 1907, it was bought by Mr. and Mrs. W. H. Borvall, according to the *Chautauqua Weekly* of May 30, 1907. There are 40 employees at the Cary, now owned by Mr. and Mrs. Richard F. Paul.

George Gershwin was a guest at the Cary in 1925 when he was writing his "Concerto in F." Gershwin was influenced to come to Chautauqua by Ernest Hutchinson, Head of the Piano Department at Chautauqua and a member of the Juilliard School faculty. The story is related that he told the clerk at the Cary desk to keep his signature on the Hotel Register because it would be worth money some day. His works are inter-woven into the Chautauqua Program each year.

Mrs. Kay Nuttal tells about coming out of the Cary with a friend on a rainy afternoon and encountering Gershwin. He asked them what they were doing and invited them to go with him. They spent the afternoon with him playing the piano. Gershwin enjoyed playing and very generously shared his talent with other people.

10 Bliss

In 1876, the site now known as 10 Bliss Avenue was leased by the Rev. R. C. Smith, a Methodist minister, for a tent. At first there was only the back part of the house (board and batten construction) which was used for the kitchen and "loft." This part still stands. Each summer a tent was erected on a platform in front of it.

In 1924, three elderly people (children of the Rev. Smith) stopped at the house and said that they had spent many summers there. They showed the present owner a picture of themselves as children seated on the stump.

The front part of the house was built in 1896. Many of the fixtures and furnishings are shown in the 1897 Sears Roebuck catalog. The front door with plain glass was listed at $4.90. The colored panes sold at 75¢ extra.

The house boasts some fine American folk art. The elaborate arch, dominating the bargeboard in the gable, frames the balcony door with its pointed doorhead. The balcony of this two-story dwelling boasts interesting spindle designs in the balustrade. These are repeated around the porch and above the porch openings.

Originally painted in typical "Chautauqua gray," it was painted white when purchased by the Denises. Now it is painted red with white trim to show up "American Carpenter craftmanship." Much of the original furniture is still used.

The Rev. Mr. Larimore C. Denise, D.D., came to Chautauqua in 1910 and purchased the property. Only a period of 10 months elapsed between the sale of the property by the Smith children and its being deeded to the Denise family. The Rev. Denise, in his chapter on Chautauqua in his "Reminiscenses" describes his feeling about Chautauqua in this way: "And thus I made one of the best, if not *the* best investment of my life. When I asked if

The carpenter's lace looks lacy and this American Gothic cottage at 10 Bliss now looks cared for and cared about.

Chautauqua was a safe place for children, he exclaimed, 'Is Heaven safe?' Our children, their children, and *their* children have played in the stream running through the ravine in front of the house." [22]

When the Denises bought the property, the inside walls were unfinished; the only lights were coal oil lamps. It was heated by a wood stove, and the only toilet facilities were in the woodshed. Later, the walls were papered, the house wired, and the bathroom built over the shed.

The house is presently owned by the Rev. Denise's daughter, Dorothy Denise Hagerman. From 1910 it has been occupied, at least for a part of each summer, by a member of the Denise family except when the Rev. Denise lived in Hawaii and the West.

65

4 Miller Park

This brown shingled house, the first house to the left of Miller Park, has a beautiful view of the lake. It is informally planned and has an asymmetrical exterior form as do true Shingle Style houses.

Built in 1900, it replaced an original tent and boarding cottage listed in 1881. Across the front is a porch which faces the area where the original auditorium was built. This porch has a white railing and posts and is covered with a roof of shingles. A peaked area is found on the second floor with two windows. To the right and a little to the rear is another area with long and narrow windows. The same type windows are used on both the first and second floors of the right side of the house.

Across the rear of the house is another unit with a peaked type roof facing each side. There are wider windows on each floor of this unit.

Stairs lead to the porch with a wrought iron railing on each side. The house is well landscaped with an open area on the right side but the house on the left is built in close proximity.

A maple panelled living room, with a fireplace at the left side, runs across the front of the house. A stairway leads to the second floor bedrooms. On the right, in the rear, is a dining room. To the left is the kitchen.

Shingle houses were found in America as early as 1840 and it eventually became quite a popular style.

Mr. and Mrs. Harold Thurston, Jr., reside in the house throughout the year.

Wythe and South Avenues
Hall of Christ

The Aula Christi (Hall of Christ), as is written over the door of this Greek Revival building, was originally dedicated for the exclusive study and worship of Christ.

This building represents the dream of Bishop Vincent, who was in Zurich, Switzerland, on August 7, 1900, when the cornerstones were laid. They each weighed one thousand pounds and came from Jerusalem. Several items of interest were placed in the cornerstones: the Bible, photos of the Chautauqua founders, a Lafayette dollar, and a daily paper among other items.

Dr. Vincent hoped the building would symbolize to the world the controlling aim and force of all Chautauqua's ministries. Dr. Arthur Bestor broadened this concept to include a social order to be realized in this.

Dr. Paul J. Pelz, designer of the Library of Congress, was the architect. He was instructed by Bishop Vincent to design a building of Greek architecture with Doric portico and transepts. Here again, we see Bishop Vincent's love for the Classical. The front facade consists of four Doric columns with a unique frieze. There are several other interesting frescoes on the extreme right and left front of the building.

The entrance to the Hall of Christ is by a set of stairs raising the portico to a level that gives dignity to the building and a view of the surrounding area, which includes the Chapel of the Good Shepherd to the left of the entrance and the Hall of Philosophy. On the right one views Alumni Hall. At the immediate right we find a parking lot and Grove.

In 1967, the Hall of Christ was completely renovated by the gifts of Mrs. Robert D. Campbell and the Gebbie Foundation. The meeting room on the first floor was refurbished. This room is used for religious services, meetings, Library Program Nights, and weddings. The small room at the left of the main entrance is in memory of Kenneth Hitchcock, once Assistant in Fund Raising. The room to the right contains the historically interesting Gould Bible Collection.

Bishop Vincent's foresight is today expressed in this imposing Classic building, and Christ's spirit lives on in this structure.

Ames and Pratt Avenues. Vincent Avenue
was cut in two to make the present Bestor
Plaza. This area is the center of
Chautauqua both winter and summer.
Here skating was enjoyed. The
St. Elmo is shown in the background.

Post Victorian Chautauqua (1902-1973)

Teddy Roosevelt is said to have called Chautauqua "The most American place in America." It may also be called "The most Victorian place in America." Much of the architecture and way of life have remained Victorian and resisted change. While it has been said countless times by both distinguished artists and vacationers, "Coming through the Gate at Chautauqua is like entering a different world," it is still appropos.

Architecturally speaking, many of the cottages remained unchanged. Some "Sawn Art" has been removed and some interiors changed to adapt them to longer seasons and more comfortable living. The old charm of the central section still prevails and the new sections have a character of their own.

No longer does one leave the horse in the stable area or arrive by the J. W. and N. W. traction at the Main Gate. One invariably arrives by car.

As you enter the Main Gate (or the smaller ones at the ends of the Grounds), you are asked to park your car across the road after delivering your luggage to your cottage or hotel. The old narrow streets still remain. This facilitates walking or bicycling, which is the wiser mode of travel.

39 North Lake Drive was built by Clement Studebaker in 1902 on property where a house built by Dr. Jesse Hurlbut once stood. Francesca G. Rappole, former Chautauqua trustee and president of the Bird Tree Garden Club, is the present owner.

39 North Lake Drive

39 North Lake Drive is historic both because of its distinctive architecture and the people who have lived there. Clement Studebaker (a Chautauqua trustee) built the house in 1902. He brought his architects and builders from Chicago. Lots 1162 and 1163 were originally leased by Dr. Jesse R. Hurlbut. Dr. Hurlbut built the original house in 1887 and it was moved a block away in 1902.

C. T. Terrill, Nina Terrill Wensley's father, purchased the cottage in 1916; she sold it to the Peters family of Oil City in 1933. Albertus Rappole became the owner in 1962, and it is now owned by Francesca G. Rappole, former Chautauqua trustee and president of the Bird Tree Garden Club from 1970 to the present.

This house has Dutch architectural characteristics. The gambrel roof extends over the front porch. There is a large picture window on the right of the porch; both give a fine view of the lake. The construction is of gray clapboard, and aluminum siding has been added.

Mrs. Rappole has added a large library and has entertained many prominent officials at her home, including former President Gerald E. Ford, who is a close friend of her brother, former Senator Charles E. Goodell. George Shearing has conducted his music workshop in this room, which contains several Maritza Morgan paintings.

The Grange Hall was the scene of a festive picnic at 8 Simpson on Grange Day in the early 1900s. The hipped roof topping this Classical type building was popular in this area.

8 Simpson
Pomona Grange (Chautauqua County Patrons of Husbandry)

The inscription on the triangular pediment above the Doric columns of 8 Simpson Avenue reads "Patrons of Husbandry." It is only fitting that Chautauqua should have a Grange, since the Grange was born in nearby Fredonia. Built in 1903, the building was presented by Cyrus Jones, prominent resident of Jamestown, as a memorial to his father, Aaron Jones.

Of Classical Revival style, the building is located on the corner of Miller and Simpson Avenues, which is one of the oldest sections of the Institution Grounds. It is just one block from the lake and two blocks from the Amphitheater and Plaza area. There are ten 4 by 8 foot round windows on all sides of the house. Steps lead up to the porch with two doors into the living room. This room was the former meeting hall and is 20 by 30 feet with an 18 foot ceiling and a large fireplace. Behind it is a kitchen, with bedrooms upstairs.

It served as the headquarters for the annual Grange Day each summer on the third day of August. Literally thousands of farmers and their families arrived in Chautauqua by wagon or boat and attended a special program in the Amphitheater. A picnic followed in the Grange yard under a tent.

The exterior of the house is covered with gray and white carpenter shingles. It is used as the home of the Edwin D. Smiths and is a perfect example of adaptive use. They have furnished the interior with colorful modern furniture.

1 Root Avenue
President's House

One Root Avenue is important because it was the home of several presidents of Chautauqua. Many distinguished guests were entertained here.

Built in Queen Anne style, it was completed circa 1905. It has the typical round tower with helmet cap on the right side of the house. The second floor porch acts as a balcony, and both porches have low balustrades. The first floor has pillars on the corner of the porch and rounded arches on the second floor. Steps with railings lead to the porch. There is a garage on the right side.

The left side of the house has a big bay window facing the lake. One finds both a double window and a fan-shaped window on the second floor. A garden facing N. Lake Drive was the scene of many gala receptions, and it was here that John Phillip Sousa gave a band concert.

There is a large living room on the left side of the house. The dining room is on the right front part of the house with a stairway from the central hall leading to the bedrooms. The house is currently painted white with yellow shutters.

Dr. and Mrs. Arthur Bestor and family made this their home during his presidency. The official entertaining for the Institution was done here. Dr. Bestor was responsible for the "Town Meeting of the Air" being broadcast from Chautauqua during World War II. Many outstanding people of world prominence were his friends. He served as president from 1915 until his death in 1944.

It was here at 1 Root Avenue that Franklin D. Roosevelt was entertained, and the wicker rocking chair in which he rocked on the porch may often be seen in the bay window of the house.

Mrs. Ambrose Cram, daughter of the Bestors, tells this tale of the strict police protection during FDR's visit to the house. She recalls that a list of everyone that stayed at the house was given to the police, but one relative was inadvertently omitted. It was a great surprise when the police tried to prevent him from entering.

The Franklin Roosevelts are among the national figures that were entertained at 1 Root Avenue when it was the "President's House."

Afterward, it became an amusing incident among this family that was so well-loved and so much a part of the Chautauqua community.

Other prominent figures entertained here during the Bestors residency include Amelia Earhart, Admiral Richard Byrd, and Eleanor Roosevelt.

The house was remodeled in 1962 when it was winterized for President Curtis W. Haug and his family. During this period most of the official entertaining was done at Packard Manor.

President and Mrs. Oscar E. Remick and their three sons lived in this house from 1971 until 1972 when 1501 N. Lake Drive became the "President's House." Chairman of the Board Richard Miller and his family then became the occupants of 1 Root Avenue. Mr. Miller is a great-grandson of Lewis Miller.

3 Packard Manor
Packard Manor

Inspired by Sir Winston Churchill's country house "Chartwell" in Kent, Packard Manor was the culmination of a dream of William Doud Packard. Mr. Packard, one of two brothers in the Packard Motor Co., built the house.

This Tudor mansion was completed in 1917. It was designed by the architectural firm of Warren and Wetmore of New York with Wililam Packard's assistance. While in a foreign land, Mr. Packard had been bitten by an insect and became totally sightless and confined to a wheelchair. He assisted the architects by arranging models of the component parts of the house, which would be to his liking, on a lapboard.

William Packard, son of Warren Packard, a pioneer in Chautauqua, purchased six and one-half acres of land adjacent to Chautauqua Institution and overlooking Chautauqua Lake. The house built on this land was to be completely fireproof. Each floor is one and one-half feet thick, of solid concrete poured on 18 inch steel girders. All walls are solid concrete, poured on 8 inch steel girders. All of the floors are covered with inlaid tile. The brick of which the house is constructed was imported from London, and the solid slate shingles, weighing an average of 36 pounds each, were imported from Belgium.

Packard Manor. This Tudor style mansion at 3 Packard Manor was inspired by a dream of William Packard, car magnate. Warren & Wetmore of New York served as architects for this elegant country house.

Mr. Packard designed an elevator, which he could operate himself, that served all four floors.

In the rear facing the lake is an 80-foot porch on the lakefront. A drive with an ornamental pool leads up to the front entrance. In addition, there are sun porches and bay windows to view the out-of-doors. Stone frames the windows of leaded panes. Twin brick chimneys rise from the many-gabled roof. In the gable over the front door is the Packard crest. Peering from a cornice of a bay window over the portal are gargoyles symbolizing music, drama, literature, and comedy.

A small tile-floored, oak-paneled outer hall leads into the large reception hall. This twentieth-century adaptation of the Tudor period is lighter in tone, expressing a revival of the Adam Period. The restoration of the Adam details was done by Harry Cox, a Chautauqua decorator, who also did work for Andrew W. Mellon in Pittsburgh.

In the spacious blue reception room we find handsome Adam details in the cornices and fireplace, one of five in the manor house. Packard Manor had its own organ. At the left is a dining room done in antique rose with an Adam frieze featuring garlands, trumpets, and urns.

Upstairs, we find 12 bedrooms and 8 baths. The most unusual bedroom has Mrs. Packard's likeness carved in the central medallion of the Adam mantel frieze.

Upon its owner's death, Packard Manor fell into various hands. Prior to 1942, the Packard management allowed the house to be used for retarded children. During that same year it was restored to a private residence by Mr. and Mrs. W. D. McCreary of New Castle, Pennsylvania. Jennie L. MacKnight, who restored the house at this time, says that Mr. Stanford White, originally sent to England to copy an English country house, revised the plans and built a similar but smaller one in Warren, Ohio.

Many famous people have been entertained at Packard Manor by Dr. and Mrs. Carl S. Winters, the present owners. Dr. Winters is moral and spiritual advisor as well as lecturer on the staff of the General Motors Corporation.

For many years the official entertaining for Chautauqua Institution was done in their gracious home. Included in this number was Ambassador B. K. Nehru of India who inscribed a copy of "Paintings of the Sultans and Emperors of India" as his thank you present. This volume is on display in the Reception Hall.

Pratt Avenue
Norton Hall

Norton Hall, a building dedicated to the performing arts, is one of the first monolithic buildings in the East. It contrasts the nineteenth-century architecture of Chautauqua with the twenties.

The building was given by Mrs. O.W. Norton, mother of Chautauqua's President Ralph Norton, in memory of her husband and daughter. After her husband lost his sight, his chief pleasure was listening to music. This was one of the reasons for the Nortons coming to the grounds.

Dedicated in 1929, it was built under the supervision of Otis Floyd Johnson with Dr. Lorado Taft as the architect. The monolithic concrete construction is embellished with sculptured decorative panels by Mr. and Mrs. Fred Torrey. They, also, did the fountain which was later moved to the front of the Post Office. Mrs. Elizabeth Hazeltine created the unique relief panels bordering the stage.

Norton Hall is within the historic Chautauqua grounds. It is located between Normal Hall on the west and Vanderbeck Chapel on the east. The seating capacity, including the balcony, is 1,367 seats.

Opera is sung here in English by the Chautauqua Opera Company. The first opera presented in Norton Hall was Flotow's "Martha" with Thomas Edison and Henry Ford in the audience. An apprentice school is held each summer. Miss Jessie Moeckel coached the opera here for over 26 years. Shirley Verett, the late Josephine Antoine and Julius Huehn, Joan Peebles, Clifford Harvuot, William Walker, Jerome Hines, and Douglas Ahlstedt have sung here.

Dedicated to the Performing Arts, Norton Hall on Pratt Avenue is one of the first Monolithic buildings in the East.

The Cleveland Playhouse presents plays in the Hall biweekly during the season. It was fortunate for Chautauqua that Frederick McConnell, director of the Cleveland Play House, was vacationing in the area when Norton Hall opened. As a result, he and President Bestor made an arrangement to introduce the company to Chautauqua, and it continues to present outstanding theater productions from an enviable repertoire. McConnell, K. Elmo Lowe, and Max Eisenstat set up a repertory theater that has given Chautauquans many delightful evenings of theater. The present director is Richard Oberlin.

Albert Stoessel, as Conductor of the Chautauqua Opera Company, gave the operatic venture an excellent foundation and impetus. This example was followed by Producer Alfredo Valenti. He preceded Julius Rudel of the New York City Opera, the late John Daggett Howell, and the present director, Leonard Treash, Director of Opera at the Eastman School of Music. Evan Whallon serves as the music director for the opera. There are frequently guest conductors who step into the pit to conduct a rewarding evening of opera.

In 1925, Mischa Mischakoff became the concertmaster of the orchestra and the Chamber Music Society was formed. Four chamber concerts are presented each season at Norton Hall. They are presented late in the afternoon on designated Mondays. These concerts continue to draw enthusiastic audiences. Millard Taylor, concertmaster with the Chautauqua Symphony Orchestra, continues to serve as director.

One of the newer type buildings, Norton Hall exemplifies the great variety of styles of architecture on the grounds. This artistic building forms the perfect backdrop for the quotation above the stage: "All passes; art alone endures."

71

30 S. Lake and Janes Avenue Chautauqua Women's Club

The present Chautauqua Women's Club House was dedicated in 1929 on the site of the home of Mr. and Mrs. Jacob Miller, brother and sister-in-law of Lewis Miller.

Jacob Miller bought what was known as the Dean's Cottage in 1880. C. D. Firestone was the next owner, and the 1895 owner, A. T. Scofield, sold it to the Women's Club between the 1917 and 1918 seasons. The "Chautauqua Women's Club," a history issued during the Chautauqua Centennial in 1974 describes it as "a many porched, yellow frame building with an abundance of full-length windows and gingerbread cornices."

In 1917, when dynamic Mrs. Percy V. Pennybacker became the president, she immediately set out to have a new clubhouse. The present one added a stately Southern Colonial Revival type architecture to the variety of styles on the grounds. Located on the lake, between the Athenaeum and

Jacob Miller, brother of Lewis Miller, bought this house at 30 S. Lake and Janes Avenue, in 1880. C. D. Firestone and A. T. Scofield later owned dwellings on this site. Mr. Scofield sold a second dwelling to the Women's Club between the 1917 and 1918 season.

the former W.C.T.U. Headquarters, it commands a fine view of the lake.

The two story high pillars with Ionic columns are topped by a pediment. A stairway with wrought iron railings lead to a porch across the front enclosed with a decorative railing. A balcony juts out over the front entrance, which is composed of double doors.

An entrance on the right hand side of the building has a doorway of Classical motif. This entrance leads into a hallway that leads to the second floor bedrooms and into the main living room. Small meetings and social functions are held in this beautiful room, which boasts a fireplace. The club's biweekly meetings are held in the Hall of Philosophy during the summer session.

The Club was founded in 1889. Emily Huntington Miller, writer, a former dean of Northwestern University and sister-in-law of Lewis Miller, was elected its first president. Strangely enough, Mrs. Miller was followed in 1896 by Mrs. B. T. Vincent, sister-in-law of the other co-founder of Chautauqua.

The Women's Club was organized for charitable, literary, educational, and religious purposes. It has worked diligently to accomplish these purposes. Indeed, it has contributed much to Chautauqua and the world. In the words of Mrs. Franklin D. Roosevelt:

"comprehensive in scope, forceful in appeal, valuable to members of women's clubs everywhere, interesting to everyone — an assembly which is not religious, social, not a civic club but a unique mosaic of all of these…a modern plane on which youth and maturity, recruit and veteran, pioneer and conservative, meet and learn from the other and both from self-disciplined masters."

The present president, Dr. E. Dorothy Dann Bullock, is prominent in the National Federation of Music Clubs which meets yearly at Chautauqua. She is a nationally recognized figure in the performing arts and was recently conferred a second honorary doctor's degree from Lycoming College.

Miller (Between Clark and Pratt Avenues)
Smith Memorial Library

Chautauquans who return year after year say they can hardly wait to return to its friendly beautiful Library. Of stately neo-Georgian architecture, it stands at one end of Bestor Plaza, set off by plantings in memory of Mrs. Walter Shaw. This perennial memorial was given by Mrs. Shaw's daughter, Louise Shaw Dill. In the back of the library is the restful Roblee Garden facing the Amphitheater.

The library is built of red brick with typical white wooden trim. Steps lead to a veranda, and you enter through double doors.

The Main Reading Room covers the first floor except for the Chautauqua Collection, which includes the archives of the institution. An open stairway behind the circulation desk leads to the second floor, where one finds the Education Library and the Creative Writing Room furnished by author Rebecca Richmond. Of great importance is the division entitled Chautauqua Heritage Museum.

Smith Library was opened in 1931. It was designed by Kidd and Kidd of Buffalo. Carl Shellberg of Jamestown was the builder. The building was given by Mrs. A. M. Smith-Wilkes in memory of her parents. They traveled extensively and collected many unusual objects of art. Two Tiffany vases, Rookwood pottery, rare books, and over 300 dolls were presented the library by their daughter.

The children of Dr. and Mrs. Arthur Bestor gave the library his collection of autographed pictures and books and other memorabilia. Thse are housed on the second floor. Dr. Bestor's funeral service was conducted in the library, the building which he helped plan and build.

The third collection housed on this floor are the papers and photograph collection of Mina Miller Edison. Many of the speeches of her father, Lewis Miller, have been included in this gift of the Charles Edison Fund. The Fund began to refurbish the Museum Room for the Bicentennial under the direction of Pauline Fancher, former Smith Librarian and former librarian of the Chautauqua Collection and Curator of the Chautauqua Heritage Museum. A lifelike bust of Abraham Lincoln by Frances Savage is displayed on this floor.

The ground floor contains the Children's Room, which was remodeled in 1968. It was given by Mrs. Clyde L. Carnahan as part of her Chautauqua Centennial gift and by Miss Helen Estabrook and her sister in honor of their parents. The renovation was planned by Librarian Pauline Fancher. The circus theme murals, inspired by antique circus figures given by William K. McKnight's children, were painted by Maritza Morgan, Chautauqua artist. Mrs. Lenore Day served as popular Children's Librarian for seven years.

The library collection contains over 24,000 books and recordings. The Chautauqua Collection has the *Chautauquan Assembly Herald* and the *Chautauqua Daily* on microfilm.

The Smith Library is one of the centers of winter activity. It sponsors weekly Program Nights, begun in 1965 under the direction of Pauline Fancher, the C.L.S.C. Discussion Groups at the St. Elmo with Barbara Bowie Haug as group leader, and classes at the library. Mrs. Torrey Isaac became the librarian in the fall of 1974.

The library site originally housed a museum which included a mummy and displays illustrating classical antiquities and the Bible.

Reading plays an important part in the life of Chautauquans, and the library is there to help them keep informed and abreast of the time in an atmosphere of happy reading.

1501 North Lake Drive

In 1972 the house at 1501 N. Lake Drive became the home of Chautauqua's president. Many of the artists and government officials presented on the Chautauqua platform have been entertained here. They include such personalities as Theodore Morrison, George Shearing, Peter Nero, Roger Williams, Gov. Malcolm Wilson, and Lt. Gov. Mary Krupsak of New York.

Walter Shaw, Vice President of the G. C. Murphy Company and Chairman of the Chautauqua Board of Trustees of Chautauqua, built the house in 1940. He and his family lived here until it was purchased by Chautauqua Institution with the help of the Gebbie Foundation. Dr. and Mrs. Oscar E. Remick and their sons were the first presidential family of Chautauqua to occupy this home.

The house commands a beautiful view of Chautauqua Lake, and there is a swimming pool on the left side of the property. Built of white clapboard, it is reached by a flight of stairs from the road.

The entrance leads to a hallway. On the left of the stairs going down to the living room is a guest bedroom. On the right is a kitchen. In front of the kitchen is a dining room. Both the dining room and the living room have a fine view of the lake. Below the first floor is a family room. On the second floor are bedrooms and the president's study. Among the impressive receptions held at this residence was the one to celebrate the Chautauqua Commemortive Stamp issued during the Chautauqua Centennial.

Rebecca Richmond, on the right, founder of the Creative Writers' Workshop and Vice President Ralph McAlister, on the left, meet at the Richmond home at 23 Haven. Beginning with Mr. McCalister, we find Marjorie Pardis, Diggory Venn, Margaret Widdemer, and Robert Francis (standing). This house, built in 1943, is contemporary and functional.

23 Haven
The Rebecca Richmond House

The Rebecca Richmond House was purchased by the Seth Goodwins in 1962. Gracious hospitality and interest in Chautauqua continues to prevail in this home planned by Rebecca or Mrs. Julian Richmond.

This house embodies Mrs. Richmond's feeling that Chautauqua should keep abreast of the times but not lose its original lofty purposes. This spirit is alive in the house, which was built in 1943 by Fay Flanders in a spot looking out on the Hall of Philosophy.

The living room has glass windows on all sides with a door in the center. More glass is being used in the contemporary houses of "new" Chautauqua. This enables people to use their cottages later in the fall and gives a feeling of being near the out-of-doors.

The house is all on one floor. The entrance on the right side leads into a hall. On the back is a bedroom and bath with a kitchen to the far left. On the right wall of the living room of this shingle house is a big stone fireplace. Over the fireplace is a copy of the Richmond coat-of-arms—a gift of some of Mrs. Richmond's English friends.

Mrs. Richmond called the cottage "Mon Abri," and it was a meeting place for writers and musicians. She started and sponsored the Creative Writers' Workshop that has continued to meet since 1946.

Rebecca Richmond also started the Bell Tower Scholarship Awards. Each year, students from England or the British Isles enjoy studying at Chautauqua under this program.

Among those who have enjoyed Rebecca Richmond's hospitality are poets Robert Francis, and John Holmes and novelist Margaret Widdemer.

When Robert Francis was asked why he did not return to Chautauqua for the workshop, he replied, "I can't imagine Rebecca without Chautauqua or Chautauqua without Rebecca."

Her son, J. Henry, and his wife, Frances, owned a publishing business in New York and lived at 6 Peck Avenue. After his death, Frances Richmond sold the cottage in 1972.

Mrs. Goodwin maintains a guest house in the rear of the Haven Avenue residence which faces South Avenue. She is very active in the Episcopal Church.

II
Second
Century

Representative Streets and Porches

Preparation for Chautauqua's second century began in 1972 when the Chautauqua Centennial Committee began our historical survey, which culminated with Chautauqua becoming a New York State Historic Site in 1973.

The survey, conducted under my direction by over sixty committee members, distributed materials and amassed and recorded the information necessary to complete the state survey forms. There are seven hundred buildings in the area inside the Institution Gate. Every street was photographed. Buffalo architect Olaf William Shelgren chose most of the houses and buildings that were submitted as typical of Chautauqua's architecture.

The survey revealed that Chautauqua has one of the nation's largest concentrations of Victorian architecture. Its uniqueness focuses on the unusual number of porches and doors that provide easy access to the out-of-doors. Those that are next described are, by necessity, but a selection of the many interesting and historically important buildings on the Institution Grounds.

Massey and Vincent. The Main Gate, of Neo-Classical style, was built in 1917. Erected as the depot for the Jamestown, Westfield and Northwestern, it presently houses the ticket offices for entrance to Chautauqua and the box offices for the Play and Opera.

Many Victorian houses may be viewed as you stroll down Vincent. Dr. Helen Overs, nationally prominent in the Episcopal Church, resides in the Hawthorne Cottage. It is the first house on the right as you enter the brick walk.

The porches of 29 Scott have many different kinds of sawn art. Built in 1903 by Mrs. Ida Baker, it was the home for many years of Grace Harger.

Pratt East. The side of the Children's School facing east has an open porch with Classic columns. The school was built in 1921 and an addition was made in 1969. One may envision the activity in front of the present school porch at Chautauqua where Nursery Education was pioneered.

1 Morris was fortunately saved by being moved when the Colonnade was built. The home of the resident physician, wooden porch railings were replaced by wrought iron. 16 Morris, the present Tally-ho, built in 1881, was the former Ohio cottage. Both 16 and 12 have a view of a ravine from the end of their porches. Louise Eve's narrow porch is enhanced by an embellished wicker settee and chairs. The Glen Park Beauty Shop at 8 Morris has enclosed porches and is owned by the Whitmores.

Note the board and batten construction of this Gothic Revival cottage at 11 N. Lake. In 1927, when a basement was being dug out under it, several Indian skeletons were found.

25 Whitfield-29 Whitfield. All the houses in this row have porches both upstairs and down. At 25, the C. Campbell Putnam home has enclosed porches. The Lucile Thomas cottage at 27 Whitfield has an enclosed porch on the second floor, but the first floor has an open columned porch. The William Miller, Jr., house has stately columned porches on the first and second levels. Beyond are Ransom, Wightman, and Patton cottages.

Miller Park has maintained its picturesque look. The cottages face a park with beautiful trees and the lake is in the foreground. The site of the original Assembly and Auditorium, it is now hallowed ground. These Gothic Revival houses are built close enough together that neighbors may rock and chat on porches. George Shearing or George Koppel may be seen strolling here now instead of Alf Landon. The first house on the left is the Miller Cottage where Mrs. Mina Miller Edison and Thomas Edison lived.

This house at 4 Miller Park, while not the typical image of Chautauqua, blends into the setting with its brown shingles and white trim. The wide porch gives an excellent opportunity for viewing the lake. The owners are fortunate in having a corner lot on Preston Street since this allows more windows and more chances for light and fresh air.

This house at 8 Miller Park was rebuilt in 1914 on Lot 26 (listed under the name of Rev. N. H. Holmes in 1888) and Lot 25. The house on Lot 25 (10 Miller Park) was taken down in 1906. The owners of 8 Miller Park have maintained the porches, the Greek Revival columns, and the delicate gingerbread. The house is now painted bright blue in keeping with one school of thought that believes color brightens up a summer colony.

Miller Bell Tower, 1911.

These houses at 8, 6, and 4 S. Terrace, are built on a bank adjacent to Vincent Avenue. The porches at 8 and 6 are on first and second levels with a space underneath. The house at 4 has a porch on the ground level and space below. All face the lake.

80

The Aldine at 20 Simpson boasts a view of the lake not only from the multi-tiered porches but from almost every window. Influenced by Richard Norman Shaw, the brilliant English architect, it combines various styles into a Queen Anne whole. Many rooming houses have numerous porches.

20 S. Terrace once was a rooming house for girls. Built in 1903 by Milton G. Twitchell, it was owned until recently by the Ward Bullocks. They made it into apartments between 1945 and 1960 and renovated the house next door, where Mrs. Bullock still resides.

On the way to the Amphitheater, at the end of Roberts Avenue, cottages and rooming houses of sawn art may be seen. All the houses have enticing porches. The Massey Cottage, the last house on the left, was built in 1880. Three generations of Masseys served on the Board of Trustees. The Massey organ in the Amphitheater, given in memory of Hart Massey, is superbly played by Chautauqua's Vice President and organist, Robert Woodside.

The cottages at 26-28-30 Miller Park (not illustrated) have many porches and doors. 26 Miller was built in 1878 by Erick Nelson, father of Laura Nelson Weaver, the present owner. 28 Miller is listed in the *Chautauqua Assembly Herald,* July 30, 1881, under the name of Mrs. B. S. Stanton. 30 Miller was erected in the form of a cross by Rev. A. J. Merchant, grandfather of Miss Jean Thoburn, Chautauqua artist. Miss Thoburn lived at 12 Cookman until her death.

William Peacock was the first owner of the property on the corner of Wythe and Miller (not illustrated). Next door is 29 Miller with wide porches on two levels on the front and side. To the left at 27 we find the Simpson Cottage, recently purchased by W. Jeffrey Simpson, prominent young Chautauqua author.

Carved lintels and decorative carpenter's lace enhance this multi-porched structure at 10 Pratt, maintained by the Reformed Church. Fredonia Cottage was believed to have been located here where J. W. Martin built this house in 1883.

Music from the Amphitheater floats over to Chautauquans as they enjoy the porches on Janes, between Clark and Wythe. Each house expresses the individuality of the owners. The Chatham, on the corner of Clark and Janes, is owned by Cecil Barr and managed by Ralph Moore. It has been kept in fine repair and is attractive and comfortable. The next house, the former Ethan Allen, has been painted bright yellow, and the railings have been changed from wood to wrought iron. 29 Janes was Mary Campbell's former summer cottage. The James Ecksteins have kept the traditional gray with white posts holding up porches on the first and second levels.

The Gingerbread Cottage begins a row of cottages with porches both upstairs and down. Built in 1891, it is elaborately decorated and is the most painted and photographed house on the grounds. Rev. Charles Foulke built his own house, as did many early Chautauquans, at 32 Janes. The next houses are part of the headquarters of the Disciples of Christ. Gingerbread trim once could be purchased by the yard, and Chautauquans embelished their porches with it.

The back view of the United Presbyterian house at 20 Janes has wide porches as well as the front on 9 Palestine. The first brick building on the grounds, it gives permanence to the Chautauqua summer colony. The garden is in memory of Mrs. Roy Mapes, a faithful Chautauquan.

The stately Chautauqua Women's Club House at 30 South Lake has classic Colonial columns that enhance its inviting porch. The "WCTU House" next door at 32 South Lake, with decorative porches overlooking the lake, is one of the most sought after houses on the grounds. To take advantage of the lake view, the houses along the Promenade have spacious porches.

The Howard Minor house, left, on the corner of Wythe and Foster still has the original porch on the side. Chautauqua President Samuel M. Hazlett, the man who was instrumental in "saving" Chautauqua in the 30s, lived at 33 Foster at one time. The shingle bungalow next door has an open porch on the right. Cliff Harvout, famous Metropolitan Opera singer, summers at 35 Foster. His two-story house has porches on both levels.

The house at 39 Janes Avenue was remodeled by Rev. Elmer Ortner. The porches were renovated and were supported by columns. The Edward Keating family of Bradford enjoy the cottage year-round. The T. H. Spellers of Buffalo are the present owners of what was originally a "Pansy" house at 37 Janes. This cottage, built by Mrs. G. S. Alden, is of board and batten construction and has wide porches. The one at 35 Janes, renovated by Clifford Cheney, Superintendent of Buildings & Grounds, for the Herman Dights, was sold in 1977 to the E. L. Jamisons.

The houses overlooking Lincoln Memorial Park at Wythe and Janes all have porches. The park, given by Mrs. John C. Lincoln and Mrs. Frank Newbury, occupies the site of the Morey Hotel. In the background can be seen the porches of the Spencer Hotel, built in 1881, and the Spencer Annex, erected in 1887.

Miller Avenue is a porch-lined avenue as we travel east. The house at 38 Miller has porches with railings and gingerbread in the peaked roof that overhang the upper porch. The one at 36 Miller, owned until 1977 by Martha and Maury Knowlton, has porches on both first and second levels. Alan E. Nelson has remodeled 32 into apartments. All of these houses were built before 1895 as shown by their listing in the *Chautauqua Yearbook of 1895*.

24 Center displays the freedom of spirit of America as expressed by the American carpenter in his Sawn Art composition. Space and light are revealed by his artistry in the porches of the house at 24 Center. The Grays, the present owners, also project this freedom.

Four houses at 40-38-36-32 Center show the variety of architecture that "openness" to the out-of-doors may take. The brown shingle style of 40 Center was very popular in western New York after the turn of the century. Miss Alice Brown, the present owner, worked on the *Reader's Guide to Periodical Literature* for many years. A one-story cottage at 38 Center has a pointed roof with Classical columns. Walcher's house at 36 Center is more elaborate and has a sense of rambling Victorian style like many larger houses on the grounds. The spacious cottage at 32 has porches in the center. Owned by Heber Harper and long-time Chautauquan L. W. Knox, it is across the road from one of the many park areas on the grounds.

Interiors

26 S. Terrace. This c. 1873 cottage living room has an air of comfort and beauty. The antique sofa and chair are combined with wall to wall carpeting.

The dining room of the Lander Cottage at 26 S. Terrace is enhanced by the elegant pull-down lamp and the glow of candlelight.

This charming desk was made by Blodgett, builder of 26 S. Terrace. The cupboards he installed in the kitchen are still in use.

The entrance to this cottage, at 20 Center, retains the early Chautauqua look. These are the stairs Booker T. Washington climbed when he stayed here. Notice the typical crockery and the container for mail on the wall.

88

This living room at 28 Miller Park was done over by Mina Miller Edison in the 1920s. The garden may be viewed through the glass doors.

Mary Valinda, wife of Lewis Miller, looks down on the living room of the Miller Cottage.

Thomas Edison's chair adjoins the fireplace of the Miller Cottage at 28 Miller Park, and a Carl Nordell painting hangs above it.

The interior of 30 Miller Park retains the feeling of the Alling Cottage with its "Gone with the Wind" lamp and chairs with caned backs and seats.

89

A "fainting couch" adds a decorative touch to the Falconer home at 32 Miller Park. Victorian ladies found these couches indispensable when they had "the vapors." Above the beautifully upholstered couch is a handsomely executed needlepoint picture.

Dainty curtains blow with the breeze in the living room of the cottage at 14 Cookman where Mary Donnelly Ritts has spent her summers. A rocker beside the fireplace and shelves with books bring a smile to Mary's face.

The dining room at 22 Center is very inviting. The oval pine table is surrounded by cane seated antique chairs. A marble top chest acts as a sideboard in this ruffle-curtained, flower-papered room.

This Bird's-eye Maple secretary was made in 1802 by Thomas Howard (or Hayward) and became the property of Margaret Dochtermann's mother. When Margaret retired she brought the desk to her parents' home at the corner of Vincent and South Terrace. The desk is pictured at her present apartment at 37 Ramble. The secretary has been willed to the Old Bridgewater Historical Society, Bridgewater, Massachusetts, and will finally return to the town where it originated.

At 22 Center Helen Theurer has kept the feeling of early Chautauqua with a characteristic rocker and marble top table. Note the decorative Welch bottle.

In 1969 the reception room of the Athenaeum Hotel, on South Lake between Janes and Bowman, was redecorated and the wicker chairs were painted blue with flowered upholstery covers. Pale yellow curtains with elaborate, candled chandeliers completed the handsome setting for gay entertaining on the grounds.

The Wensley House at 22 S. Lake has been tastefully redecorated by a group of dedicated young Chautauqua women. The dresser on the left was of a style popular in the cottages on the grounds.

The bedroom at 26 N. Terrace has a typical spool bed, washstand, and mirror. Grandma Ward's picture hangs above the dresser.

The bathroom of this 1881 house at 14 Cookman was decorated by Mary Ritts, TV entertainer. Orange, green, and white brighten the drab interior. Notice the original walls of the entrance with an unusual wicker door for ventilation.

When is a door not a door? One of the intriguing touches of the Howard Minor Cottage at 33 Foster is a door marked "Original Back Door." It leads to a closet containing a refrigerator. The Foster Avenue side of this house is still in its original condition.

This washstand at 45 North Lake, in the home of the George Cornell family, was used by President William McKinley when he visited here. The President was a close friend of Lewis Miller and came here often to visit his aunt, Mrs. Osborn, at 17 North Terrace. The Institution provided him with a fine carriage.

The windows on the stairway landing at 32 S. Lake have colored glass in diamond patterns. The walls of the living room are covered with wainscotting.

The old pine walls at 34 Janes Avenue lend a mellow glow to the living room. The Victorian sofa with a pieced coverlet invites you to tarry. A typical shelf holds a Seth Thomas clock, hand-turned candlesticks, and other memorabilia of Chautauqua highlights.

The Victorian platform rocker and chair (said to be from the Athenaeum Hotel) are covered with red velvet. The Gone-with-the-Wind lamp was a Larkin premium and belonged to my grandmother, Huldah Alden Waters. Mrs. Waters came to the Chautauqua Assembly in a horse and buggy with her father, the Rev. Israel H. Alden, a Baptist preacher ordained in the Methodist Church.

The Kimball back porch at 23 Morris has a beautiful view of the Ravine. This is a bird-watchers' paradise.

This is the Kimball Collection of World War I blue and white china. This china was sold at the Pier and was popular in the cottages.

Ruby glass souvenirs of Chautauqua are displayed on the Karslake's dining room table. The grandchildren's doll is waiting to be served by the fireplace.

The Karslake kitchen view shows the round tube above the towel rack. The Karslake's grandchildren can talk into this tube to tell how they want their eggs cooked.

This desk was used by Mrs. G. A. Alden when she wrote the "Pansy" books. It is made of typical walnut with curly maple trim so popular in Victorian Chautauqua. Mrs. Alden owned 37 Janes Avenue. The present owners, the T. H. Spellers of Buffalo, have blended new with old to make a pleasant interior.

Two spectacular pieces of furniture on the grounds are found in the home of Doris Goodrich Jones at 19 Emerson. Of all the wicker rockers on the grounds, the one pictured is most unusual. The epergne holds Doris' favorite things, and the stand was made at the Arts and Crafts School by her Aunt Henrietta Jones.

95

All the Adam friezes have been restored in Packard Manor and add to the pleasure of being entertained in the dining room.

The fireplace with the Adam decoration is the focal point of this bedroom in Packard Manor. Carl Winters' aunt painted the still life, and the doll was given to Mrs. Winters by a lady in a nursing home who wanted it to have a good home.

The organ at 3 Packard Manor has been replaced by an antique piano, but the pipes still decorate the alcove of the living room. The organ is now enjoyed in the Hall of Christ.

Mrs. Pennepacker seems to cast an approving glance on this formal living room in the building at 30 South Lake Avenue she helped build in 1929. Fireside chairs in blue and white welcome guests to the fireplace decorated with delicate candelabra.

The candelabra at the Women's Club was left them by Mrs. Arthur Bestor, wife of Chautauqua's president. Above the table is a painting by Betty Geddes, Chautauqua artist and author of children's books.

People

People taking advantage of the principles, ideals, and surroundings have made Chautauqua what it is. Many of them are mentioned previously in this book. I regret that I lack room to include more.

This part covers but a few of the people that stand out over the years. They are but examples of the characteristics with which true Chautauquans are endowed.

We salute these individuals that embody any or all of the qualities of the Chautauqua "idea." May future generations strive for the same ideals.

It is difficult to name the common characteristics that outstanding Chautauquans possess. Those that come to mind are a pioneer spirit, courage, devotion, tenacity, humaneness, faithfulness, originality, and talent. The people mentioned display one or all of these. They combine the spiritual, educational, and cultural objectives for which the Institution stands.

As I intimated in the preface I'm inclined to see Chautauqua through rose-colored glasses "for now we see through a glass darkly and now face to face."

I believe that Chautauqua ideals are worth striving for, that the historic Chautauqua architecture is worth saving, and that Chautauqua's greatest asset is the wonderful people that return year after year.

Frances Willard was enshrined in the hearts of Chautauquans by a memorial window in the Anne M. Kellogg Memorial Hall. Presently it is on display in the WCTU headquarters in Evanston, Illinois. A popular speaker at the first Assembly, she pioneered the causes of women's suffrage and temperance.

Burt Mustin, of television fame and a lifetime Chautauquan, is pictured second from left with his eyes on the future Mrs. Mustin. The group is standing in front of the banner of the Pierians, the name of the CLSC Class of 1890. The Chautauqua, Literary and Scientific Circle, the first Book-a-Month Club in America, together with the Chautauqua movement provided an international outreach with the message of Chautauqua.

The Hukill and Clark families are pictured at the sandpile in front of the Hukill cottage at 38 S. Lake in 1894. From right to left are Mrs. N. Clark, Mrs. Hukill, and Mr. Hukill. All the Clark and Hukill children are shown with their two governesses.

Teddy Roosevelt poses in the doorway of Higgins Hall on August 19, 1899, with Jamestown author Jacob Riis and Chancellor John H. Vincent.

Ida N. Tarbell, author of a four-volume *Life of Lincoln* (1895), received early newspaper training on *The Chautauquan.* A "muckraker," her inquiring mind dates from her early association with Chautauqua. She commented in her autobiography, *All in a Day's Work,* that "the sound of hammers nailing together…flimsy cottages was never stilled."

Jane Addams gave some lectures on modern problems of family and social life as early as 1893. Bishop Vincent is among those honoring her, in 1915, when the CLSC Class was named after her.

Mrs. Grassie, faithful CLSC member, relaxes with friends in Pioneer Hall. On the mantle, left to right, are pictured Kate Kimball, Jesse Hurlbut, and Mrs. B. T. Vincent.

Margaret Miller Newman, daughter of Ira Miller, eldest son of Lewis Miller, presents additional bells for Miller Bell Tower for the Miller family in 1967. A lifetime Chautauquan herself, Margaret is noted for her gracious entertaining and her fascinating stories about "Grandfather" and Chautauqua. The presentation took place atop Sample Playground erected in 1966 on Miller Park.

Chautauqua sets aside one day a year to honor libraries. "Library Day" is celebrated with a program sponsored by the Friends of Smith Library. In 1967 Thyra Ferre Bjorn, famous Swedish-American author, was our speaker. She is shown in the Library doorway with Gerald Heglund, who arranges "American Scandanvian Day" at Chautauqua each year. Coming out Smith Library door is Marjorie Bertram Smith, who for many years was poet in residence at Chautauqua.

101

Karl Menninger, famous psychiatrist, is a favorite speaker at Chautauqua. Here he poses for Revington Arthur, Director of the Art Department.

Mrs. Howard Hanson, wife of the emininent composer, is the owner of this house built in 1920 at 10 North Lake Drive. Mrs. Hanson's mother was a patron of the arts, and they entertained many distinguished musicians at their home. The site was formerly occupied by a house covered with sawn art built by Glidden of Cleveland, founder of the paint company. It was listed in the *Chautauqua Yearbook of 1895* under the ownership of Frank Higgins of Olean, donor of Higgins Hall.

102

Edwin Prince Booth autographing "A Tribute on the Ninetieth Birthday of Albert Schweitzer" which he helped edit and which he reviewed for the CLSC, for Helen Theurer, CLSC Director, 1966 to 1970. They are pictured on the porch of the "Verandah," a charming Victorian house at Clark and Bowman that serves as offices for the CLSC. Weekly "Sidewalk" sessions are held from the porch.

Mrs. Nately Ronsheim, the Director of the Chautauqua Literary and Scientific Circle, lives at 30 Miller Park. She is holding a glass which says "Alling" on it. Formerly a rooming house, the "Alling" has been made into apartments. Mrs. Ronsheim has blended the old and new in her apartment. Edison slept here when courting Mina Miller. He taught her the Morse Code on the lake. Later he tapped a proposal to her on her hand in code and she tapped "yes" in return.

The *Böse Mädchen* (angry litle girl) is the name given to Margaret Robinson Dochterman's portrait painted by German artist Altuber. The artist escaped to Estonia and since Margaret's father, George didn't have time to sit for his portrait, she was designated. Margaret had to sit rigid and he would scream at her if she moved. This shows in her facial expression in the portrait.

Pauline Fancher, the "Lady from 34 Janes," was the chairman of the group responsible for seven hundred buildings and houses being added to the National Register of Historic Places. Here she rocks on her tent-platform porch.

104

Madam Shao Fang Sheng teaches and shows her jewelry at the Chautauqua Art Association Galleries on Wythe Avenue. She delights Chautauqua audiences with her Chinese philosophy. A student of Frank Lloyd Wright, she is at home teaching cooking, art, jewelry making, or singing. Trained as a painter and musician in Peking, she and her husband won a five-year scholarship to study architecture as apprentices. In her art demonstrations she shows her technique with swift beautiful brush strokes.

Doris Goodrich Jones came to Chautauqua to study violin and stayed to delight children of all ages with her puppets. She is shown in her cottage at 19 Emerson in front of the fireplace. The small painting on the left side of the mantel is by Will Smedley, and the umbrella stand on the right is the work of Henrietta Jones.

Mrs. Frank Falconer was at home summers in her Chautauqua cottage at 32 Miller Park until her death in 1977. Her winter residence was in Winter Park, Florida. This gracious hostess exhibited her doll collection on an antique sofa.

Bess Shephard Clayton Morrison summered with her Grandmother Shephard at 12 S. Lake and has been responsible for bringing many prominent speakers on crime to Chautauqua.

Much of the Institution's entertaining has been done in this stately mansion, Packard Manor. Here we see Mrs. Alice Winters, wife of Dr. Carl S. Winters, Public Relations Representative for General Motors, standing on the stairway. Notice the exquisite finials atop the stairway railings. Mrs. Winters is active in civic affairs.

Mrs. Mary Kimball Haker pictured in her wicker chaise at 23 Morris Avenue. The Kimball cottage has a large variety of wicker pieces. Mrs. Haker, a life-long Chautauquan, was president of the Bird, Tree, and Garden Club from 1957 through 1960.

105

Katherine King Karslake gazes at a picture of her Grandmother King in front of the windows at 44 South Lake Drive. A long time Chautauquan, Katherine helped research the houses for the Historic Site nomination.

A duchess of Czechoslovakia by birth, Maritza Morgan met her future husband, a doctor, at Cornell University. They purchased a cottage at Chautauqua. Since her husband's death she has been a year-round artist in residence. Her burned painted bas reliefs were featured on the "Today" show in 1974. She is also the author of a children's coloring book, *Chautauqua, I Love You!*

Florence Tan, Instructor in Chinese at Chautauqua Summer Schools, made this picture which says "I love you" in Chinese. It hangs in the living room at the Disciples of Christ Headquarters at 36 Clark Avenue.

We welcome our fourteenth president to the grounds. Dr. Robert Hesse will take up residence as president of Chautauqua on January 1, 1978, and will occupy offices in the Colonnade building. Dr. Hesse is familiar with the rich heritage of the institution as he lived in Fredonia when he was Assistant to the President of Fredonia State College. He served as Assistant Director of the Chancellor's Panel on University Purposes for the State University of New York from 1970-71. From then until 1974 he was director of communication services for the American College Public Relations. That year he became President of Medaille College in Buffalo. He, his wife Barbara, and their four children will reside at "Lakeview," the President's home at 1501 North Lake Drive, Chautauqua.

Conclusion

Now that Chautauqua is in its second century it is time to reevaluate its past. We have seen in this book our evolution from our primitive beginnings. We have progressed from portable tents to permanent brick structures. Our faith in the continuance of Chautauqua is shown by the durability of the houses and buildings.

Chautauqua has become a center of cultural wealth. Paul Malo, western New York architectural authority, in *Landmarks of Rochester and Monroe County* says: "Buildings become more than facts of history; they are to be read as expressions of people who built them, varying from the simple folk art of rural cottages and mills to the urbane subtleties of cultivated taste."

This book tries to make you aware of the whole of Chautauqua as well as the significance of individual buildings. Chautauquans feel very close to this place, and I hope this book makes the reader see our familiar surroundings in a newly appreciative way.

Chautauqua is worth preserving. Our guests come yearly to see its unique character. I hope that this book has helped you understand "the Chautauquaesque look and idea" and that you will rededicate it to posterity.

My hope for Chautauqua was best expressed by George Vincent in his 1901 report to Chautauquas' Board of Trustees:

The Problem of Chautauqua Enthusiasm

At the risk of seeming to obtrude sentiment into a business report, the principle of instruction ventures to point out a danger and to urge a necessity.

There is a danger that Chautauqua may become merely a successful resort, thought of by friends and the public as a business enterprise. This conception of Chautauqua would be fatal to its permanence and success. The only hope of growth and extension in usefulness lies in regarding Chautauqua as an institution and in rallying an enthusiastic following about its standard. Appeal cannot be made on the basis of denominational loyalty, but surely the history of Chautauqua and the possibilities of the idea can be counted upon, if only all the friends of Chautauqua insist to themselves and to others upon the true point of view. Endowment must be secured; buildings must be erected; the work in all departments must be extended. These things are possible only to those who have loyalty, faith, courage and persistence. Let the motto for the new century be, "Chautauqua an Institution and an Ideal" — not a business and a summer resort.

George E. Vincent (1901)

Notes

1. J. T. Edwards, *The Silva of Chautauqua Lake* (Meadville, Pa.: Chautauqua-Century Press, 1892), p. 12.
2. Rudyard Kipling, *Abaft the Funnel* (New York: B. W. Dodge, 1909), p. 188.
3. Ibid, p. 201.
4. Helen P. Jacox and Eugene B. Kleinhams, Jr., *Thousand Island Park: One Hundred Years, and Then Some* (Thousand Island Park, N.Y., 1975), p. 49.
5. Charles Lock Eastlake, *Hints on Household Taste in Furniture, Upholstery, and Other Details,* American ed. (1872).
6. Daniel D. Reiff, *Architecture in Fredonia* (Buffalo, N.Y.: Thorner-Sidney Press, 1973), p. 62.
7. A. J. Downing, *Cottage Residences,* 2nd ed. (New York: Wiley & Putnam, 1844).
8. Chautauqua Collection, Margaret Copeland, Librarian, 1962.
9. Ibid.
10. Jesse Lyman Hurlbut, *The Story of Chautauqua* (New York & London: G. P. Putnam & Sons, 1921), p. 163.
11. *Chautauqua Assembly Herald,* August 18, 1876, p. 4.
12. *Chautauqua Yearbook for 1895* (Meadville, Pa., Chautauqua-Century Press, 1895), pp. 31-35.
13. *Chautauqua Assembly Herald,* July 24, 1889, p. 2.
14. Chautauqua Collection, Vincent Letters, from Frances Willard, October 9, 1876.
15. Jesse Hurlbut, *The Story of Chautauqua* (New York & London: G. P. Putnam & Sons, 1921), p. 148.
16. Edwin P. Booth, CLSC Recognition Day Address, 1966, pp. 6, 8.
17. Floyd L. Darrow, *History of the Town of North Harmony,* Book 1 (Stow, N.Y.: Town Board of North Harmony, 1953), p. 5.
18. Chautauqua Collection, Chautauqua Abstract Search for 28 Miller Park.
19. *Chautauqua Assembly Herald,* August 9, 1977, p. 1.
20. *Chautauqua Daily,* August 4, 1971.
21. Ben Karp, *Wood Motifs in American Domestic Architecture: Phantasy in Wood* (New York: A. S. Barnes & Co., 1966), p. 86.
22. Rev. Larimore Denise, *Reminiscences* (Chautauqua Historic Sites Survey, 1973).

Glossary of Architectural Terms

Adam: Robert Adam details gave interiors creative and personal touches daintily and exquisitely executed in a light and quick rhythm. Moldings often included Adam-like urns and garlands.

arcade: A range of arches based on piers or columns.

asymmetrical: Unbalanced proportions.

balloon framing: The horizontal members are nailed to the studs or uprights that run from sill to eaves.

banding: Any flat thin strip or molding.

balustrade: A row of posts in a series topped by a rail.

bell hood: A projecting covering in the shape of a bell that throws off the rain above an arch, doorway, or window. Also called a hood-mold.

board and batten: Narrow wood strips covering the joints of vertical wood siding.

bracketed: A projecting weight supported by a piece of stone or other material.

campanile: A bell tower, often separate from a main building.

capitals: The head or crown of a column.

criss-cross: Lines or, in Victorian architecture, strips of wood crossing each other in different directions.

clapboard: The horizontal boarding that covers the side of a wooden house with overlapping or tapering of boards.

cupola: A dome or small structure above the roof of a building.

Doric: The simplest column of the three classical orders.

eaves: The under part of a roof projection overhanging the wall to carry water away from it.

entablature: The upper sections of a wall or story usually supported by columns or pilasters.

finials: Any crowning ornamental architectural detail.

gables: The vertical portion of the end of a building from the cornice level or eaves to the ridge of the roof.

gambrel roof: A roof having its slope broken by a greater than right degree angle.

gouging: To scoop out with a concave-convex cross section.

helmet cap: A cap resembling head armor in shape, position, or covering often at the top of a column.

hipped roof: A flattened pyramid in form, with roof planes sloping in four directions.

Ionic: One of the three orders of classical columns identified by its scroll-like capital.

lintels: Covering of an opening made by a horizontal beam or stone bridging.

mansard roof: A roof with a double pitch on all four sides, the lower steeper than the upper, associated with the Second Empire of France.

monolithic: Any structure formed by a single piece or block as of stone.

mullion: A vertical division between windows or panels.

oriel: A large bay window often supported by a bracket.

pavilion: A moveable or open structure for temporary dwelling.

pediment: The triangular space forming the gable above a horizontal entablature in a classical style building.

"Picturesque": Interesting dispositions of forms and variety of texture in buildings or landscapes.

portico: A columned porch with an entablature.

quoins: Blocks, usually stone, laid at the corner of a building.

sawn art: Architectural embellishment of a home or building by use of a saw.

stick style: Pieces of wood arranged in a pattern symbolizing the structural frame in vertical board and batten siding.

stringers: Any horizontal framing timber.

turret: A small and slender tower-like structure.

vernacular: Dwellings made of kind of stone or wood used locally.

vergeboard or bargeboard: A board, often ornate, attached along the rafters of a gabled roof.

Victorian: Relating to the period of Queen Victoria from 1837 to 1901.

wainscoting: A narrow wooden paneling or a similar covering by another material.

Bibliography

Alden, Isabella MacDonald ("Pansy"). *Four Girls at Chautauqua.* Boston: D. Lothrop, 1876.

Bestor, Arthur E., Jr. *Chautauqua Publications: An Historical and Bibliographical Guide.* Chautauqua, N.Y.: Chautauqua Press, 1934.

Bisbee, Mariana M. *Tent V.* Boston: D. Lothrop Co., n.d.

Booth, Edwin P. *Booth Speeches.* Chautauqua Collection, 1966.

Bruch, Kate P. *Early Days of Chautauqua.* Canton: August 1, 1897. Chautauqua Collection, 1977.

Butler, Joseph T. *American Antiques 1800-1900.* New York: Odyssey Press, 1965.

Chautauqua Abstract Searches and Deeds. Chautauqua Institution Vault, Chautauqua, N.Y., 1977.

Chautauqua Assembly Herald. Chautauqua, N.Y. 1876- . Chautauqua Collection, 1977.

Chautauquan Daily. Chautauqua Collection, Chautauqua, N.Y., 1977.

Chautauqua Historic Sites Survey, 1973. Chautauqua Collection, 1977.

Chautauqua Women's Club, Chautauqua, N.Y., 1974.

Chautauqua Year-book for 1895. Meadville, Pa. The Chautauqua-Century Press, c. 1895.

Conover, Jewel H. *Nineteenth-Century Houses in Western New York.* Albany, N.Y.: State University of New York, 1966.

Copeland, Margaret. Notes. Chautauqua Collection, 1977.

Darrow, Floyd L. *History of the Town of North Harmony.* Book 1. Stow, N.Y.: Town Board of North Harmony, 1953.

Denise, Rev. Larimore *Reminiscences.* Chautauqua Historic Sites Survey, Chautauqua Collection, 1973.

Doty, William J., Ed. *The Historic Annals of Southwestern New York.* New York: Lewis Historical Publishing Co., 1940.

Downing, A. J. *The Architecture of Country Houses.* New York: Dover Publications, Inc., 1969.

Downing, A. J. *Cottage Residences.* 2nd Ed. New York: Wiley and Putnam, 1844.

Eastlake, Charles Lock. *Hints on Household Taste in Furniture, Upholstery, and Other Details.* American Edition, 1872.

Edwards, J. T. *The Silva of Chautauqua Lake.* Meadville, Pa.: Chautauqua-Century Press, 1892.

Explore Chautauqua Walking Tour Guide of Chautauqua Institution. Chautauqua, N.Y.: Friends of Smith Memorial Library, 1974.

Fleming, John; Honour, Hugh; and Pevsner, Nikolous. *The Penguin Dictionary of Architecture.* 2nd Ed. Baltimore: Penguin Books, 1975.

Gould, Joseph E. *The Chautauqua Movement.* New York: State University of New York, 1961.

Harrison, Harry P. *Culture Under Canvas.* New York: Hastings House, 1958.

Hazlett, Samuel M. *Diamond Jubilee Pageant, Chautauqua Through the Years.* Jamestown, N.Y.: Chadakoin Press, Lafayette Press Inc., 1948.

Hendrick, Ellwood, *Lewis Miller.* New York: G. P. Putnam's Sons, 1925.

Hitchcock, Henry-Russell. *Architecture, Nineteenth and Twentieth Centuries.* Pelican History of Art Series Baltimore: Penguin Books, 1958.

Hurlbut, Jesse Lyman. *The Story of Chautauqua.* New York & London: G. P. Putnam & Sons, 1921.

Irwin, Alfreda L. *Three Taps of the Gavel: The Chautauqua Story.* Westfield, N.Y.: The Westfield Republican, 1970.

Jacox, Helen P. and Kleinhams, Eugene B., Jr. *Thousand Island Park: One Hundred Years, and Then Some.* Thousand Island Park, N.Y.: 1975.

Karp, Ben. *Wood Motifs in American Domestic Architecture: Phantasy in Wood.* New York: A. S. Barnes & Co., Inc., 1966.

Kipling, Rudyard. *"Chautauquaed,"* in *Abaft the Funnel.* New York: B. W. Dodge, 1909.

Maass, John. *The Gingerbread Age.* New York: Bramhall House, 1957.

Maass, John. *The Victorian in America.* New York: Hawthorn Books, Inc., 1972.

McKee, Harley J. *Recording Historic Buildings.* Washington, D.C.: Department of Interior, 1970.

McMahon, Helen G. *Chautauqua County, A History.* Buffalo: Henry Stewart, 1958.

Malo, Paul. *Landmarks of Rochester and Monroe County.* Syracuse, N.Y.: Syracuse University Press, 1974.

Mayville Assessors Records. Mayville, New York.

Morrison, Theodore. *Chautauqua: A Center for Education, Religion, and the Arts in America.* Chicago: The University of Chicago Press, 1974.

The Old House Journal. Field Guide to Old House Styles. Brooklyn: The Old House Journal Co., 1974.

The Old House Journal. The Domestic Architecture of Downing. Brooklyn: The Old House Journal Co., 1974.

Orchard, Hugh A. *Fifty Years of Chautauqua.* Cedar Rapids, Iowa: The Torch Press, 1923.

Reiff, Daniel D. *Architecture in Fredonia.* Buffalo: Thorner-Sidney Press, Inc., 1973.

Richmond, Rebecca. *Chautauqua, An American Place.* New York: Duell, Sloane and Pearce, 1943.

Richmond, Rebecca. *Invitation to Chautauqua.* Chautauqua, N.Y.: Chautauqua Institution, 1953.

Schmidt, Carl F. *The Victorian Era in the United States.* Scottsville, N.Y., 1971.

Simpson, Jeffrey. "Utopia by the Lake." *American Heritage* (August 1972).

Sprague, Paul E. "Lincoln Park: A Notebook of Architectural Types." *Nineteenth Century* (September 1975).

Vaux, Calvert, *Villas and Cottages.* New York: Harper & Bros., 1857.

Vincent, John Heyl. *The Chautauqua Movement.* Boston: Chautauqua Press, 1886.

Vincent, Leon H. *John Heyl Vincent, A Biographical Sketch.* New York: MacMillan, 1925.

Vincent Letters. Chautauqua Collection, 1977.

Warren, R. M. *Chautauqua Sketches: Fair Point and the Sunday School Assembly.* Buffalo: Otis, 1878.

Wells, B. Jeanette. *A History of the Musical Festival at Chautauqua Institution, 1874-1957.* Washington, The Catholic University, 1958.

113

Index

117